Lee R. McMurrin, Ph.D.

Stories from the
FRONT LINES
of
INTEGRATION

TOLEDO, OHIO 1965–1975
and MILWAUKEE, WISCONSIN 1975–1987

Copyright © 2014 Lee R. McMurrin

Cover and book design by Thomas Osborne

Distributed by IngramSpark

All rights reserved. No part of this book may be reproduced, stored in a retrieval system, or transmitted in any form, or by any means, electronic, mechanical, photocopying, recording or otherwise, without prior written permission of the author. Permission to use articles and commentary in the appendix must be obtained from the respective media sources.

Library of Congress Control Number: 2014917090
ISBN: 978-0-692-27589-4

Printed in the United States of America

*Dedicated to the memory
of my beautiful and talented wife,
Frances M. McMurrin, who provided
a well-decorated and lovely home for the family,
going from one school system to another,
following her own dedicated and
creative attributes.*

*And to the parents,
both black and white, who volunteered
to send their children to a school
of their choice.*

Acknowledgments

There are two outstanding school administrators who guided me through my maturing years in school administration.

Dr. Paul C. Hayes, as school superintendent, hired me as a fifth grade teacher in Sharonville, Ohio. After one year and a few months, I was drafted into the US Army during the Korean War. Upon my return, he asked me to join him as his assistant in a school system with four schools. We were the only full-time administrators. I followed him for 12 years as he went to various sized school districts. He was a great friend and mentor to me.

In 1965, I joined Dr. Frank Dick as he took on his first superintendence in a major city during tumultuous times. He never spared an experience that would prepare me for my future years in school administration. I believe he gave me excellent recommendations to the board members from Milwaukee that helped me get that position as superintendent, confirming that I was ready for that opportunity and challenge. He contributed so much to the successes I had in my 12-year tenure in that position.

The most extensive editing was done by Gary G. Hall, a classroom teacher in the Kent School District, Kent, Washington.

The completion of this book is attributed to professional help from Louise Hawker, who put it all together. In particular, she edited the script, organized the chapters, arranged the photos, arranged and listed the items in the appendices, and coordinated its publication.

LEE R. MCMURRIN

Foreword

McMurrin Legacy to Schools Record of Commitment, Hope

Lee McMurrin came here with impeccable credentials and he left with the same: his spirit and reputation unscathed, his enthusiasm undiminished, his moral purpose undaunted by the petulance of some of his colleagues, the posturing of some of his bosses, the blistering – and sometimes steamy – censure of some of his critics.

He came with a charge and he left with its challenges met: as in magnet if not metropolitan, as in desegregated and democratic if not perfectly integrated (as if he could magically change the landscape and play monopoly with neighborhoods and make saints of those who still thrive on division.)

He came without malice and left, after 12 years, without malaise: a gentleman, thoughtful and, to a flaw in the world of petty politicians and nay-sayers without portfolio, with the courtesy of the patrician he never betrayed. He was one of us, a hard-working, socially consumed, deeply concerned citizen laboring now in the trenches, now at City Hall, now in the classroom, now at the state house, now in the board room, now and then on the vita course at Lake Park.

He came with a resonant and calming voice, a voice more eloquent and wise than picayune and shrill, if sensational, stylings of those who still regret that Reynolds decision and those who would rehearse Plessy vs. Ferguson, retreating into some never-never land where education is left to the vagaries of attitude by educators with political lesson plans.

He gave our kids hope and their parents a dose of the reality that made them players. He gave our city a distinction it may not recover, however staunch the search; a place in the delivery of options unparalleled and eagerly imitated in those places where knowledge, courage and freedom are preferred to another century of variations on the McGuffey Reader.

We liked his smile and the grit behind it, his style and the soul behind it, his campaign and the character behind it, his patience and the principles that remain the cornerstone of Milwaukee's public schools.

RABBI FRANCIS BARRY SILBERG
From a submitted editorial in the Milwaukee Journal
(now known as the Milwaukee Journal-Sentinel),
October 31, 1987. Used by permission of Rabbi Silberg

Praise for **Stories from the Front Lines of Integration**

Lee McMurrin takes no prisoners in presenting a real world picture of the nasty elements and inhumane character of an urban city and how one man can make a difference. From the unfortunate attitudes of business leaders, civic notables and union bosses, to the likes of the White Citizen's Council, Nazis, and Ku Klux Klan, we begin to perceive the struggle to educate a citizenry in what democracy is all about and McMurrin's personal destiny when he accepted an urban superintendency. Lee McMurrin was well schooled through his trials by fire in a previous urban setting and ready, willing and able to pick up the torch and lead a city through the treacherous path of institutional and personal racism. This treasure trove of anecdotal vignettes lays bare the soul of prejudice and racism within a city, and the trials and tribulations of this heroic leader.

This would truly be a collection of woeful tales from a crypt of white pride and prejudices, and black shortsightedness, save for the character of one human soul whose resilience and stamina kept an urban complex's head above water. A good read into what it takes to be an urban superintendent in the race-oriented world of today.

Understanding that any racial integration process required a successful first phase —the desegregation process—Lee McMurrin was able to accomplish what a series of local Doubting Thomases needed to see: Successful Desegregation. The background of what Milwaukee was able to see was violence in Louisville, Denver and Boston. Extra reporters were hired to report on the anticipated violent reaction to a federal judge's order to desegregate a very segregated city, but all they had to report was, largely, success stories.

This is an excellent read for college courses in leadership and administration, as well as an excellent subject for book clubs and other community leaders on how to handle difficult people in a world of race baiters, closet racists and persons steeped in personal prejudice.

It was a real pleasure to serve with Lee McMurrin as a city wide elected member of the Board of School Directors.

LEON TODD
former member, Board of Directors, Milwaukee Public Schools

Contents

CHAPTER ONE
A Brief History of School Segregation and Racial Prejudice in Educational Institutions
1

CHAPTER TWO
Attitudes on Race:
Toledo, Ohio Public Schools 1965-1975
7

CHAPTER THREE
Attitudes on Race:
Milwaukee, Wisconsin Public Schools 1975-1987
31

CHAPTER FOUR
A Case for a Voluntary Approach to Integration, Using Educational Incentives
83

CHAPTER FIVE
Leadership Style and Management Principles
93

CHAPTER SIX
Perspectives on Busing
103

CHAPTER SEVEN
Responses to the Stories from the Frontlines of Integration
127

APPENDIX
132

CHAPTER ONE

A Brief History of School Segregation and Racial Prejudice in Educational Institutions

"Prejudice is a burden that confuses the past, threatens the future and renders the present inaccessible."

MAYA ANGELOU

Abraham Lincoln said many times, in his speeches and debates on slavery, that if slavery is not wrong, nothing in this world is wrong. And I was quoted many times saying that segregation was the worst thing that ever happened to America's children. Slavery of the "colored people" (the term commonly used in earlier times) in America is the backdrop to segregation in all of its forms. Slavery formed the attitudes upon which segregation was established. Slaveholders viewed the colored people in the same category as animals, which was the way the Supreme Court of the United States viewed them in some of their decisions. Lincoln, in his debates with Steven Douglas, stated that they were human beings and should be granted the rights and privileges that were granted to citizens of the United States in the documents of the founding fathers.

As a young man, Lincoln and a young friend took farm produce on a barge down the Mississippi River to New Orleans. It was there that he saw for the first time black Africans chained to posts, being examined as you would farm animals ready for sale. He never lost this image of inhumane treatment in his mind and pledged to do something about it if he ever had the opportunity.

Before the Civil War, the US Supreme Court ruled that slaveholders could take their slaves, cows, horses, and all their property, including their black mistresses, into the newly formed states in the western territories. Abolitionists found this abhorrent, expanding the slaveholding states beyond the original set in the South. Some of the founding fathers thought that slavery would die off over time if it was confined to a set of states in the South.

It is obvious that, even after the terrible Civil War and the Emancipation Proclamation, the former confederate states would work diligently in every way to restrict the rights of the colored population by passing laws to keep them separate in all aspects of life. The US Supreme Court helped to keep and perpetuate this doctrine by establishing the policy of Separate but Equal. This doctrine, adopted by the highest court in the land, flowed from the Plessey vs. Ferguson case, which applied directly to segregated coaches on passenger trains. But this case was used to justify those laws and customs that segregated all aspects of social life, including schools. There was a jurist on the case who wrote the minority opinion, believing that this decision would cause racial unrest in America that would last more than a hundred years. That prediction turned out to be true. He also observed that white coaches and colored coaches separated and restricted the freedoms of citizens of the United States, but Asians, who had most recently been declared by Congress as non-citizens, were permitted to ride in either coach.

The attitudes that supported slavery were consistent with the attitudes that supported segregation. African Americans were thought to be inferior to white Americans and, when separated by race, the African Americans were placed in an inferior position, which perpetuated the superiority feelings of white Americans.

This affected the lives of children who were growing up in this unfavorable position. They began to believe they were inferior to others. Therefore, on many occasions in my presentations on the need for integration, I expressed over and over that segregation was the worst thing that ever happened to America's children. The segregation laws were strictly enforced to keep the races separate, but the equal part adopted by the court was never enforced or even observed. There were individuals who tried sincerely to make situations equal, but it was impossible to make it happen. Separate is never equal.

For example, during the 1960's I had numerous opportunities to observe school situations in the South. On one occasion in southern Georgia I was given a tour of a rural county and its new school construction. I first saw a school bus coming down a country dirt road. The front fenders were loose and flopping up and down as the bus went over bumps in the road. It was very noisy with an engine that was not hitting on all the cylinders and the muffler must have been damaged. This was the bus that was transporting black children to their new school. Then came the well-maintained school bus transporting white children to their new school. The bus looked like it was new and went quietly over the bumpy country road. This was obviously separate but not equal treatment.

I subsequently visited the new school, at the invitation of my father-in-law, built for all the white children in the county. There were separate buildings for primary, intermediate, middle and high school programs, all on one campus. The design was modern with color and construction appropriate for the different grade levels. The buildings were constructed of brick with overhangs and cement walkways and driveways with curbs and blacktop pavement. The landscaping was lacking, which would have added to the beauty of the site, but maybe that was to come later.

The school for white children had a paved road in front of it. We traveled far enough down this road to experience a dirt road so we knew we were now in "colored town." At a short distance, we saw an area with a large sawmill and a very prominent stack of sawdust. Across from the mill was the new school built for all the black children in the county. It was very small, with maybe four rooms built out of cement blocks and a tin roof. There was no sign of paint in or around the school and the furniture in the classrooms was made up of assorted colors and styles of used kitchen tables and chairs. I asked how this could be equal to the separate facilities for white children. The answer was common, because I had heard the likes of it before. I was told that these children don't like school; in fact, they don't regularly come to school and drop out as soon as they can, so why spend tax money on them when it is only wasted. The separate schools were not equal and, in their minds, there was justification for it.

Conditions for separate but equal, which were intrinsically unequal, were common in the South, which was the result of de jure segregation—segregation by law. But conditions which may not be as stark as the example given above were present in the North, which was the result of de facto segregation. Racial prejudice was not confined to the South. As I will point out in the stories from my own experience as a school administrator in two Northern cities, these prejudices caused individuals and groups to take positions that promoted the separation of the races, which resulted in unequal treatment of school children. On a number of occasions I heard the same justification for the unequal treatment: that this would be a waste of the taxpayers' money and some legislators would recommend cutting the state support of city schools.

Slavery provided the attitudes that became the backdrop to segregation and the attitudes which it perpetuated. One cannot enslave another human being without it affecting your way of thinking and the attitudes which follow. It is well known that a feeling of superiority existed among the white population, and feelings of inferiority were instilled in the minds of the minority population. It's unfortunate that these attitudes still persist today among some people and, in particular, children. The CNN TV channel ran a series on this subject, in which black children examining dolls thought the black dolls were not very bright, and also were more akin to being violent. It is so unfortunate that these feelings still persist in America.

In the 1950's the Supreme Court reversed the doctrine that had been upheld for nearly 100 years, which was the separate but equal doctrine. This was challenged in the Brown vs. the Topeka Kansas Board of Education case. They ruled that separate was inherently unequal, and that changes should take place. The changes came very slowly, which reminded me of Lincoln's reference to his general in charge of the Potomac army, General McClellan. General McClellan, in spite of all the reinforcements, would never move against the fortress in the South, Richmond Virginia. He commented that General McClellan had "slow," as if it was a disease or an inherent trait. The South, after this ruling, was behaving with "deliberate slow," so that the Supreme Court ruled that they should proceed with "deliberate speed." The changes still came slowly, but surely. Because of similar attitudes which were prevalent in the South, there was segregation in the North, which is known as de facto segregation. In the first case, de jure means by law; in the case of the northern part of the country, it was "in fact" segregation.

In this book I am presenting experiences that I had in two major cities in the North dealing with biases in the integration of schools: first in Toledo, Ohio, 1965–1975; and subsequently in Milwaukee, Wisconsin, 1975–1987.

CHAPTER TWO

Attitudes on Race:
Toledo, Ohio Public Schools, 1965-1975

"The humiliating expectations and traditions of segregation creep over you, slowly stealing a teaspoonful of your self-esteem each day."
MELBA PATILLO
African American Student in Little Rock, Arkansas

Introduction

While the South was struggling with the dismantling of segregation, the Northern states were facing the possibilities of a federal court case for the segregation that existed in most large cities.

There were groups such as the NAACP and others who brought complaints to boards of education, and eventually to the federal courts, that the schools were segregated. There were groups and organizations on both sides of this question, such as the John Birch Society, the Ku Klux Klan, and the White Citizens Councils, that were geared up to fight the efforts taking place to dismantle segregation in the public schools. It seemed that even more moderate individuals and groups were compelled to take sides in these cases. These were volatile times for school systems, particularly in large cities.

In 1965, I was interviewed by the newly-appointed school superintendent in Toledo, Ohio, a major city school system comprised of more than 40,000 students and a minority population of approximately 33 percent. Through several interviews it became very apparent that we shared the same small-town values, even though I was about three years younger. We both came from small high schools in a rural county, south of Toledo. We both went to the county basketball tournament at Bowling Green State University in Bowling Green, Ohio while we were in high school. We were both involved in small town community activities. He had enlisted in the U.S. Army upon graduating from Cygnet High School and was almost immediately in the Battle of the Bulge in World War II, where he was wounded. During the war, I was 16 years old and went to work on the C&O Railroad in Walbridge, Ohio. I was hired as a night clerk, but went to high school during the daytime.

We both worked our way through college, and very quickly went through the steps to be top school administrators.

The superintendent was formerly the superintendent of the Sylvania Public Schools, which was a very upscale suburb of Toledo. He was very successful there. I was assistant superintendent in the largest suburban school system in Ohio, which was outside of Columbus. In the summer of 1965 I was hired to become the assistant superintendent of Toledo Public Schools.

To reinforce the idea that we were both on the same page, I told him during one of the interviews that there was a sign on the lawn at the central office that said, "This is not a playground. No children allowed." That hardly seems appropriate for a school system. At the next interview, the sign was gone.

Our first task was to do everything possible to address the problems of segregation in order to stay out of federal court, as well as to bring greater opportunities and education improvements to both black and white children.

That fall, he was very interested in implementing the Lighted

School House program, patterned after the program in Flint, Michigan. This initiative opened up the schools as community centers for children and adults. One of the controversial introductions was roller skating on gym floors. At that time, there were special skates that could be used on hardwood floors, so no destruction would come to the hardwood surfaces. I must say this was one of the most popular activities for young children to learn to skate and participate in such a wholesome activity.

Also that fall, the superintendent presented to the board of education a policy on education and human rights. This policy stated that the school board was committed to eliminating all policies which tended to segregate the children and to form policies that would help to integrate black and white children in the Toledo Public Schools. After this, the first policy statement brought to the school board was a procedure to allow the minority/majority transfers. It was called the majority/minority pupil transfer system. This allowed for minority students to apply to fill empty seats in majority white schools. The reason it did not work the other way was because the "black schools" were filled to over capacity. We also developed career skill centers at each of the seven high schools in order to attract the exchange of students. In this case, they could go full-time or part-time to the high school with the career skill center of their choosing.

It became very apparent that there would be staff resistance to these policies, which is illustrated by the following stories.

Attitudes of Staff Toward Policy Changes

Teacher Declares She Will Not Teach Black Children

In an upscale neighborhood where the school was nearly across the street from the University of Toledo, two black students were assigned to a fifth grade classroom. The teacher announced that she would never teach a black child in her classroom. She played sick, week by week, during the school year. She called in each Friday to declare that she would be out sick for the next week. This procedure was allowed by the union contract.

Toward the end of the year, the teachers' union held their annual banquet. The superintendent and the deputy superintendent customarily sat at the head table. But on this occasion they were seated at a two person table in the far corner of the room. Everyone was waiting expectantly for the announcement of the union's pick of the teacher of the year. Much to our shock and surprise, the teacher of the year was the fifth grade teacher who declared she would not teach a black child. The Toledo Education Association was not a supporter of the majority/minority transfer policy. So in this case, they registered their protest.

Attendance Officer is Angry
About the Results of the Transfer Policy

On the first day of school, an attendance officer visited an upscale, majority white high school. She came charging into my office and past the secretary. Pounding the desk, she said, "This high school is ruined." She said she saw black children in the halls, in the classrooms, and in the office. They were everywhere. Black students had taken over the school. Since I had approved all of the transfers to this high school, I knew the numbers were small. I pulled out the records and told her that the percent of black students was less than five percent. She declared that I was lying, that she saw it firsthand. She wanted me to admit that the school was now a majority black school, which meant that it was ruined.

Union Custodians Misunderstand Racial Unrest

From time to time, there were protests organized to march on public buildings in order to disrupt their operations. Since we were so close to Detroit, and Detroit had many disturbances, these marches sometimes influenced groups in Toledo, which was a very quiet city. When I would hear about these rumblings of marches on schools or on the administration building, I would personally go out to meet the group and to answer all their questions and protests, in order to prevent the disruption of the school's peaceful operations.

On this particular day, I left the office and instructed two custodians to man the doors, which had safety locks. I instructed them to let our staff in and out, but when the protestors arrived, they were to keep the doors locked. I met with the protest group and prevented their march on the administration building. But when I returned, the custodians had locked the doors and left their assignment to monitor the two exits to the building. I searched for their presence, and upon finding them, they said they were on their lunch break. They pulled out the union contract, which gave them the right to have their lunch at a particular time. Therefore, they walked away from their duties, which posed a highly dangerous situation in which the safety locks were on the doors and the staff could not safely get out of the building.

The Death of Scott High School

The assistant principals of Scott High School came to my office with the proposition that we should have a ceremony to bury the symbols of their high school. These included things like their motto, mascots, school flag, and accreditations, since the school had become all black, and was no longer the school that it once was. In other words, this was the death of Scott High School, and a ceremony would bring closure to that fact. It was a terrible idea.

I told them that we're not abandoning Scott High School, and we are going to work hard to make it one of the finest schools in the city.

White Principal Bites Black Kindergarten Child

I was meeting with a small group in my conference room and a staff member, who was in charge of security, knew that he could interrupt me at any time if there was a disturbance which needed my attention. He came into the room and whispered in my ear that a principal had bitten a kindergarten child and the parents had organized a protest. I said, "Investigate that, and I will soon close off this meeting and make a call to the principal," which I did. I asked her if she bit a kindergarten child, and she admitted that she did. I said, "Why did you do that?" She wanted to teach the child that it hurt when you bit someone. I asked her how things were going at her school, and she said, "I've been having many problems."

I told her, "I'm sending over a principal to take charge of your school," and asked her what she saw, as a professional, to be her future. She hesitated a bit and told me she would like to be a school psychologist. I did not assure her of this opportunity. However, she was given another assignment, but not as a principal, and a riot was prevented.

Study of Black History

Late in the 1960s there was much discussion of teaching black history in colleges and universities, as well as in public schools. It was noted that this history was lacking and, during these times with so much black and white tension, it was important to have a solid understanding of history. So this was a national discussion, which appeared in major newspapers and monthly magazines, such as Time and Newsweek. Since it was being widely discussed, I brought teachers of social studies from junior and senior high schools into the central office auditorium to openly discuss this subject. I was very direct in telling them where I stood, which was that we should include references to the black experience and black heroes as they naturally would appear in history. At this meeting, some teachers protested that they would not teach black history.

In other words, they took sides. But I told them they didn't have a choice, that they should bone up on the subject and be ready to make solid historical presentations to students. The teachers went back to their schools, some of them in the protest mood, and generated criticism of the policy which I had presented to them. Hearing some of this, I went to Woodward High School and visited social studies classes, and took questions from the students. A student of Polish descent said if we teach about blacks in American history, why don't we teach about the Polish? I mentioned to him several Polish heroes, particularly during the Revolutionary War, which he and all the students should have been aware of, so no ethnic group should be neglected.

Reactions of Governmental Agencies

Governmental agencies were perplexed during these times, not knowing exactly how to respond. Here are some examples:

State Legislature Passes Resolution

One evening the Ohio State Legislature passed a resolution stating that no more state funds should flow to the Toledo Public Schools because they were now a Communist cell. This came about as a protest to the special federal grant we received to teach both Chinese and Russian language and culture. In fact, it was called the Sino-Soviet Studies Center. One of the graduates of this program became a contract lawyer for General Motors, and was involved in their negotiations with China for trade agreements. In other words, this was a very valuable contribution to America's security and leadership in the world. But the State Legislature viewed it in a different fashion, thinking it was a Communist cell. However, it was a resolution that had no ill effects on the Toledo

Public Schools. The State money still flowed to the school system as prescribed by the law.

State Legislature Annexes Black School District to Toledo

Late one evening, the State Legislature passed a law annexing a very small black rural school district to the Toledo Public Schools. This was done in order to avoid litigation that the state had participated in policy and practice to isolate a black population. In other words, there were numerous consolidations of small school districts which this rural district could have been a part of, but the state purposely skipped over them and left them isolated and segregated. The district was about 20 miles away from Toledo. I think I made the first visit to our newly acquired schools, which was one elementary school constructed from unpainted cement blocks, and a new high school which, in some cases, looked very modern in its construction. The elementary school smelled like a sheep shed and the high school was missing ceiling acoustical tile. The former superintendent told me that the board president had sold the tile in order to have some cash in the school district's accounts.

There were numerous stories about bringing these schools into the Toledo school system. One Monday morning I had a call from a nearby school superintendent, saying that the high school basketball team did not show up on Saturday night. I called the school to find out what the circumstances were. After some investigation, I was told that the team forgot that there was a game, and forgot to go. My comment was, "Didn't you have a pep rally? Didn't you have practices preparing for the game?"

I received no legitimate answers. Also, I had a call from a farmer who had ridden his tractor and equipment by the high school, and the flag was flying upside down. He wanted to know if that was a signal that the school was in distress. The school was somewhat in distress by some measures, but in this case the custodian had raised the flag upside down.

Title I and the Welfare Mothers

In 1965, we were applying for funds under Title I of the Elementary and Secondary Education Act. We had filed our application with the State of Ohio, which included education improvements that had come to schools with a majority of students from poverty-stricken homes. There was a national organization of welfare mothers that had lobbied the Department of Education for funds to provide general welfare to poverty-stricken families out of these educational funds. I was called to come to Columbus, Ohio to meet with officials to discuss our application, which had already tentatively been approved. I was surprised that we were meeting with the Federal Director of Title I, who at that moment disapproved of our application, which centered on educational programs. I asked him, "OK, how should we spend this money?" He said, "Buy food and clothing."

I learned later that he was not an educator but an accountant, and had little background in educational endeavors. The meeting closed with no agreements, but I stated that we were not going to spend this money on food and clothing; that should be taken care of by the welfare department.

Libraries in Elementary School Disapproved

In our application for Title I funds, we had about ten educational improvement projects; one was developing libraries in schools that had a concentration of poverty. The state approved our application, including the library project, but the federal government disapproved of the libraries, and other parts of our application. I went to Washington, DC to persuade them to approve our libraries, which I thought were very important contributions in areas of the city which were poverty-stricken and with limited access to books, newspapers, and magazines. I went to a large building where I think the room number was in the thousands. I found a lady who approved or rejected applications for libraries. She was an educator from New England and I explained to her the need for these libraries in the elementary schools. She understood from our application that we were asking for a second library, believing that every school had a library (to begin with). In fact, she even explained that in New England they built a library and surrounded it with classrooms. I told her, in the Midwest, we often build a gymnasium and surround it with classrooms. She now understood that we had a legitimate case to bring libraries into our elementary schools, and she approved the project.

Meeting President Johnson in the Rose Garden

President Lyndon Johnson could actually be called the education president. He was responsible for implementing the Elementary and Secondary Education Act, and Head Start, among others. He was very concerned with the war in Vietnam, but remained optimistic that the war would come to an end, and when it did, there would be 43 billion dollars available to improve America's public schools. So I was invited, with about 20 others, to the White House to spend the day discussing recommendations that the President could use to present to Congress. So he met with us briefly in the Rose Garden, gave us our assignment, and hurried off to another meeting. At the noon luncheon, Vice President Hubert Humphrey spoke to us. When he took the podium, the head table fell into the participants with salt shakers and sugar bowls and plates going everywhere. Humphrey remained unfazed, but the Secret Service quickly surrounded him and protected him from any chaos that might ensue.

He then resumed his speaking. He very calmly greeted the participants and told a story from his experience at the Maine State Fair. He was the keynote speaker, and the first elected Democrat that they'd ever had speak to them. As soon as he took the platform, it fell in. So we picked up some humor from this occasion.

Understanding the Tense Environment in which School Systems Operated

In these times, school districts had to deal with reactions and protests, which were reflected in the attitudes and actions of many organizations and groups. School systems had to operate in this tense environment. It was widespread. These are stories that illustrate and give substance to an understanding of this environment.

Black Children Can Have Lice Also

During these times, the school board meetings were very active and, sometimes, very tense. The leader of the P.T.A. spoke to the board about the problem of white children coming to school in the fall and having head lice. The school system, which she said always favored black children, ignored the problem that white children were having with head lice. She was very upset. In the ensuing discussion, the school board president, who was a prominent black lawyer in Toledo, stated that black children can have head lice also. The headline in the paper the next day was, "Black Children Can Have Lice Also." So this certainly indicates equal opportunity!

It didn't come out in the discussion over lice, but white children often go to camp during the summer and share combs, brushes, and pillows, and become infected with head lice. Most black children in poverty cannot afford to go to camp, so they do not have this experience.

War on Poverty

President Johnson initiated the federal program known as the War on Poverty. Each community had to form committees to organize ways to eliminate poverty. It generated a lot of dramatic energy in the black communities of large cities. A group in Toledo organized a street rally, during which they reported they had invited the school superintendent and other city officials to speak.

In this case, they had not notified the officials, and the residents who showed up for the rally were disappointed and angry. They organized another rally, and it was announced that I would attend the rally and answer all their questions and concerns. I was escorted into a tavern that had a second story conference room, which would hold maybe 20 people. It had microphones and speakers directed toward the hundreds of residents who assembled outside. It was as if I was stuck in this room, since the staircase was so narrow that I could hardly navigate from the first floor to the second, and I wondered how I would ever get out of this place. I was able to respectfully address the crowd, and answer their questions and address their concerns. It turned out to be a very peaceful event, but back at the office the security staff treated me like a warrior who had just returned from battle. They were happy that I survived. On the outside, these occasions are always perceived to be more dangerous than they actually are when you appear on the scene.

Bias in Churches

During this period in our history, there was a struggle in schools to be integrated after the 1954 Supreme Court case, Brown vs. Board of Education, Topeka, Kansas. This case required the dismantling of separate but equal school policies in the South, and eventually called for dismantling segregation at restaurants, theaters, and all public facilities. However, most churches persisted, particularly in the South, in having separate worship services for blacks and whites.

I was in Fairbanks, Alaska having coffee at a restaurant where it was 60 degrees below zero outside. There was frost on door casings, and on all of the windows inside. After getting my first cup of coffee, a man came in and sat down at the table, which is customary in Alaska. We opened up a conversation as to why we were there in the winter time. I was there on a mission with the Methodist church to offer encouragement to members of the congregations who were depressed from the long, dark winter. The gentleman who joined me was the former pastor of a prominent church in the South, and the only Southern Baptist church he could find to pastor was in Fairbanks. The church officials had denied him any pastorate of any Southern Baptist church in the South. This was because of racial biases and racial tensions at this time in our history.

One Sunday morning, at his Southern church, a well-dressed black couple came up the steps to enter. The ushers rushed to the pastor who was having prayer with his elders to see if they should let them in for worship. He said, "Yes. Have them come in and be seated." He told me that, as he opened the service that morning, he mentioned that this couple was welcome. In the history of this church, black and white families came together and sat in the same pews, so this was not so unusual. Well, in the recent history of this church, it was an unusual situation. The tensions between blacks and whites were so great that the elders held a secret meeting. That morning the pastor was dismissed from that church, and was unable to get a pastor's position in any other church in the South of that denomination. It is not unusual to observe that, during these times, people were adamant in taking sides. Either they were for equal rights or they were against it.

Sit-down at Scott High School

Early one morning, I noticed students fast stepping on the way to school, and they were being given leaflets as they approached Scott High School. This alerted me to believing that something was going on, and it may need my attention. I quickly went to the principal's office, and found the pastor of a local church with a group of students, who had the flyer in hand. The flyer had a list of demands, a sit-in was called for after the second bell, and they should assemble in the first floor of the foyer. I instructed the secretary to turn off the bell system after the first bell rang, and began to work on these demands with the delegation that had shown up. We were very close to agreements, or at least some satisfaction on the demands, when the second bell went off. A secretary came into the office and saw that the bell system was off, so she methodically turned it on. The local pastor quickly took off running down to the foyer. Earlier, I had told him that what he was doing was very dangerous, that it was a three story building with two open stairwells, and we could very easily have students pushing and shoving. A terrible accident could take place, and I was holding him individually responsible. He came back breathless, saying, "They won't listen to a thing I say!"

Of course, I could have predicted this. When 2,000 students show up and fill two open stairwells, the foyer is full, and they have no idea why they are there except the second bell rang, you would just have a lot of confusion and noise. A staff member and I left the room, and went down to announce to the students that they should return to their classes. We did this on a one-to-one basis. The students were wonderful; they returned to their classes, probably wondering what in the world was going on. A lady teacher rushed out of her classroom to take my arm and said excitedly and anxiously, "What should I do now?" I said, "Do you have students in your classroom?" She said, "Yes." I said, "Why don't you teach them?" She said, "Wonderful idea," and returned to her classroom.

Martin Luther King Jr. Speaks at Scott High School

One evening Martin Luther King Jr. came to speak for the first time in Toledo at a community gathering, where the most important people in the city had comments to make before he had a chance to speak. I took my two daughters with me, and people were kind enough to give us comfortable seats. We weren't on bleachers, we were on regular seats. The field house was packed, with standing room only. After at least ten speakers, Martin Luther King Jr. had a chance to speak. The reception was respectfully rousing, with lots of applause and verbal response. This was his first visit to Toledo. The Toledo superintendent called the superintendent of schools in Cleveland to see what effect Martin Luther King Jr.'s visit would have on our schools and the city. He told him that his numerous visits to Cleveland were always constructive and helpful. Dr. King's visit did not have an impact on Toledo.

Woodward High School Student Walkout

I received a call from the Woodward High School principal stating that there would be a story from his school tonight on local television, that a local TV channel had taken rolls of film of students passing from classroom to classroom between periods. Since I had been alerted, I watched that channel and they opened the local news by saying, "Student unrest had moved from the college campus to the high school and Woodward High School was in the midst of a protest," which showed up on the film they had made. Of course this alarmed the parents of these students and the residents in the vicinity of Woodward High School. Keep in mind that the unrest on college campuses centered on protests of the Vietnam War, and did take place on numerous campuses throughout Ohio and the United States.

This newscast set fire to many tensions which already existed, and caused Woodward High School to be closed for several days in order to avoid violence, which was appearing on almost every corner. Residents sat on their porches cradling long guns. In order to bring some semblance of resolution in the community so that we could safely open Woodward High School again, we invited about 40 influential members of the community to join me at the high school one evening to discuss the many tensions, most of which had become racial. There must have been 25 police dressed in riot garb surrounding the high school in order to protect the group that was to assemble. At the meeting, I had someone helping me put items on a chalkboard, and I asked the assembled group, point blank, "What's the problem?" The first statement was that the principal was a problem, and we had to get rid of him. We went down a long list. One father of students said that if we could hear the conversation around the dinner table, we could never peacefully open the high school again. Someone suggested that it was the newcomers to the community, which referred to black residents. A black representative said that his family had been there for six generations; he didn't feel like a newcomer. It should be noted that he wore an African garment known as a dashiki. I think he wore this for the effect that it might have on white residents. Others suggested that it was Eastern Europeans who had recently immigrated to this country and had taken up residence in the Woodward High School area.

I asked for volunteers to join me on Monday morning as we opened up Woodward High School, to monitor the situation, and who would be able to authentically report back to their constituents on how things went. I believe about five individuals joined me and the opening went smoothly. I mentioned to them that the school is overcrowded by about 800 students, and we need to develop more classroom space. One observant individual said that the present enrollment must be the capacity since all the students were there and none were being pushed out into the yard. Therefore, we didn't need to build more classroom space. But when they changed classes, and the halls were packed, he changed his mind.

Father Groppi Comes to Toledo with His Milwaukee Commandos

A few days later, after the visit of Martin Luther King Jr., Father Groppi, a Roman Catholic priest and Milwaukee, Wisconsin civil rights activist, marched down the streets of Toledo with his Milwaukee Commandos. The Commandos were an all black male group formed by the NAACP Youth Council to help protect marchers and Father Groppi during freedom marches in that city. These commandos carried clubs like paddles. The parade was very peaceful, but some students took note of the commandos' behavior, and mimicked them at a school assembly at Scott High School. Scott High School had a well-organized assembly with students in small discussion groups reviewing a series of questions that would bring their ideas and diverse thinking together. This was reported to the entire student body by student leaders assembled in the field house. The principal gave them instructions on how to leave the field house, and what the rest of the day's schedule would be, and they were dismissed. However, at the two exit doors were students dressed like the commandos, with clubs fashioned in the same way that they had observed on the street. I breathed a prayer, praying that I hoped we wouldn't have a lot of violence, because most of the students would take exception to this behavior on the part of these young men. After a very successful and peaceful assembly, it could have ended up in violence. As the students pressed against the exit doors, the young men acting as commandos finally gave way, and let them pass into the halls without any hindrance, and then to their classrooms. It is after occasions like this that you breathe a sigh of relief, and, of course, develop a high respect for these children who held steady during a very critical moment.

Black Panthers Invite Local Pastor to Be Their Chaplain

A news article appeared in the paper with a picture of the newly organized Black Panthers marching down a main street carrying long guns. Later that week, I got a call from a local black pastor who said he was now the chaplain for the Black Panthers. During the discussion I warned him that he will be mistreated as a chaplain, which I had learned from contacts I had with organizations like this in Chicago and in East St. Louis, Illinois. I got a call from him after a few weeks saying that I was right. They had him pinned against the wall in his church office, demanding that he do something at the end of a gun. He told me that he would no longer be their chaplain. I learned later that this was an ad hoc organization. They were not governed by the national organization of Black Panthers.

White Citizens Council Meetings

Almost weekly, the White Citizens Council would meet with me to go over complaints they had about racial problems. I believe the first meeting was on the subject of black history. They didn't want black history taught in American history classes; they wanted it overlooked as it had been historically when they were in school. During these times, there were national discussions on the subject of black history, which was often neglected by teachers and professors in American history classes. The White Citizens Council was now aware of these discussions and tensions where people took sides. On other occasions they were concerned about black and white children going to school together, and protested that they didn't want any mingling of black and white students. In other words, they should sit on different sides of the classroom, and not be involved in physical education activities where they might have to hold hands. They never got much satisfaction from me on these complaints, but came back time and time again to express them to me. Finally, they gave up on me.

Response to Martin Luther King Jr.'s Assassination

As soon as the breaking news included the assassination of Martin Luther King Jr. in Memphis, Tennessee I began to think about what impact this might have on the schools and what the situation would be like the next morning. Early that morning I began to tour inner city schools. My first stop was at a large elementary school, where I interviewed a black principal and asked for his opinion on how the students might respond to this terrible news. His first response was that his students wouldn't know who Martin Luther King Jr. was. This might sound so unusual, but at that time Martin Luther King Jr. had only been to Toledo once, without much fanfare, and he was not a prominent figure in the minds of inner city school children at that moment. Later, that would all change, with much attention given to the assassination, as well as the contributions that Martin Luther King Jr. had made to the black community and to the nation.

Bias in Sports Events

When our team took the floor at a basketball game against an all-white suburban team, you could feel tension. At a tournament game in a suburban high school, the athletic director had placed the locker room for the suburban team under the bleachers of the city fans. The locker room for the city team was under the suburban fans' bleachers. Therefore at half-time, empty soda cans were thrown on our team, along with sacks of popcorn. Of course this was a very foolish move on the part of the athletic director who developed the logistics for the basketball tournament. Also, he had invited the deputy sheriffs to provide security and, at half-time, the deputy sheriffs were scattered in front of the city school fans, but none in front of the suburban fans. This was another point of racial tension, but the city fans did not adversely respond, and just sat quietly observing this racial affront. We were prepared for any disturbance by having our own security, which was made up of former star athletes in uniform jackets, which could quickly respond to any unrest. Therefore, we were pleased that our fans behaved peacefully without incident. I was told that there were individual incidents after the game with fans confronting the deputy sheriffs in the parking lot.

Girl Track Star

A young black girl was winning all of the events at the Toledo Blade Relays. This came to the attention of the school board, and they wanted to have her recognized, as we recognized other outstanding students at the regular school board meetings. So she appeared at a regular school board meeting, and the school district's athletic director presented her to the school board and told of her outstanding achievements. Now the school board got into a discussion, with some wanting to know who her coach was. The athletic director said she didn't have a coach. At her high school, they had recently lost their girls' track and field coach. The school board had just passed a policy that said that you had to have a certain number of athletes in a particular sport in order to support a coach. There were two women board members who were very agitated by the fact that this young lady didn't have a coach, so they wanted a coach appointed immediately. Other board members took the position that if she's winning every match even without a coach, why should we spoil her with a coach. I instructed the athletic director to make sure the boys' track and field coach gave her the attention she needed to participate fully in high school track meets.

Concluding Comments on the Front Lines of Integration from 1965–1975

These stories don't stand alone but are part of a long history of integration efforts coming out of the Brown vs. Topeka, Kansas Board of Education case. The next two stories took place in the 1950s, which illustrate the innocence of citizens in the North to what was taking place in the South, and also were reflected in classrooms in the North.

They Have Colored Water Here

My family took its first trip south to visit their three sons who were in the military service during the Korean War. Arriving at the rest stop at Look Out Mountain in Tennessee, my youngest brother, age 14, came back announcing to his older brother, who was 16, that they had colored water here. So the older brother,

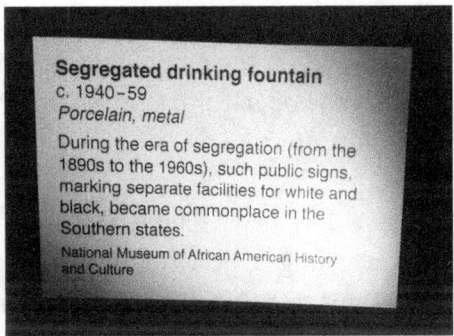

During segregation, fountains in the South were labeled white only and colored only. These photos of this relic of the past were taken at the Smithsonian Institution in Washington, D.C.

knowing the situation in the South said, "Let's go check it out." They found that the line for white water was very long, but no one was lined up for colored water, so they tried it. There was such a loud uproar from the long white line that two guards came out of the rest stop and escorted the two boys back to the car.

This was not the end of the story. When they entered the lift to go up to Lookout Mountain to see four states, they sat in the back of the lift, seeing that this bench was vacant. The operator would not engage the lift to go up the mountain since my brothers had sat on the bench that was reserved for colored people. He told them to get off the lift so the others could go up the mountain. They didn't understand completely what was going on, and they stayed on the bench. Finally the operator gave up and took the group up to the top of the mountain. Upon arriving, he stood at the door to protect the boys from an angry crowd, since they had broken the protocol of separation of the races. Going down the mountain, they still sat on the empty bench at the back of the tram, and apparently the operator had given up on these boys from the North, without protest.

Marching Behind the American Flag

As a young supervisor of elementary schools, I visited many classrooms to become acquainted with the curriculum and teaching techniques at each grade level. Therefore, I visited first grade classrooms to learn more about elementary education, as it took place at the beginning. Here is an example of practices which stem not only from racial differences, but also attitudes relating to the poor. I could cite many examples, but this is one that stands out in my memory.

In the early 1960s, I visited a first grade class in Dover, Ohio and saw their opening exercises. It included the playing of "Stars and Stripes Forever" and children holding a well-sharpened pencil with a clean handkerchief, all marching behind the American flag. In the seats were some children, who, the teacher told me, came from the other side of the tracks. They were never able to pass the health inspection, which consisted of a fingernail inspection and the sniff test, or have a well-sharpened pencil with a clean handkerchief. I asked her how she felt about this, and she said for years she noticed this, of course, and felt awfully bad, but she didn't know what to do about it. So I said, "Why don't you get a box of well-sharpened pencils and a box of Kleenex and have these kids put a Kleenex over a well-sharpened pencil." That way they could join the parade and march behind the American flag and feel like they were a part of the American dream.

America's school children should always have equal treatment within the public school's classrooms. But the atmosphere surrounding the school didn't always provide a positive atmosphere, even in the North. The atmosphere of prejudice prevailed for too long and was difficult to eradicate. There were just too many strongholds of prejudice.

The small changes made in the Toledo Public Schools were enough to keep the school system out of federal court. Then I moved to a school system that was already in federal court and was waiting for the judge to rule on the case in the Milwaukee Public Schools.

CHAPTER THREE

Attitudes on Race: Milwaukee, Wisconsin Public Schools, 1975–1987

"To live anywhere in the world today and be against equality because of race or color is like living in Alaska and being against snow."
WILLIAM FAULKNER

Introduction

In the spring of 1975, I was being interviewed by the fifteen-member Board of Directors of the Milwaukee, Wisconsin Public Schools. I was one of two finalists under consideration. We were making the rounds, being assessed by the Parent-Teacher Association, the media, community leaders, and teachers' unions, as well as the personnel committee of the board. One of the finalists was the superintendent of schools in Providence, Rhode Island, and the other was a deputy school superintendent in the Toledo Public Schools. The Providence Public School Superintendent had experience going through a federal court order to integrate the schools. The Ohio deputy superintendent had worked with the superintendent in Toledo to stay out of federal court through a voluntary approach to the integration of schools. This was very successful. The Toledo public schools were able to stay out of court. The board selected me.

The case in Milwaukee had already been tried. Everyone was waiting for the judge's decision, and thought surely he would decide the case when the new school superintendent arrived.

In order to get acquainted with the Milwaukee Public School system, I was invited to their biannual May Day music extravaganza. After being hired to take office on July first, I was warmly welcomed to a city-wide music festival that was part of the May Day events. The sports arena floor was filled with a 400-member band and an orchestra of several hundred for this enormous event. The stands were filled with several thousand elementary age students and 15 high school choirs, all in their colorful robes. One side of the arena was full of enthusiastic parents, friends and school personnel. This gave me a glimpse of what a large city school system can do when they all work together. What an expression of talent and organization.

During the concert my wife, Frances, was in conversation with school administrators' wives. She was advised not to send our children to the Milwaukee Public Schools. The women stated that our family's tradition, which was to live in the city and send our children to the nearest public school, was not a wise thing to do.

This conversation was reported to the principals at the first principals' meeting, because I was not happy with that kind of attitude on the part of our administrative staff. I told them they might be captain of a ship, but that they were part of a fleet: the Milwaukee Public Schools. We had a long way to go in improving the schools, and I needed the full support of the administrative staff.

On June 29 I was introduced to the 15 members of the Board of School Directors and the regular attendees at the monthly meeting of the board. Early that fall the board sponsored an official civic welcome at a reception in a large ballroom at a downtown hotel with the mayor and other notables on the platform. My parents

At the May Day Music Festival, several thousand children were involved in various activities. The Superintendent is directing a 400-member band in "Stars and Stripes Forever."

came from Iowa to join in this event, and they sat at a table with a gifted school superintendent who hired me in my first teaching position, and for whom I worked for at least twelve years in small Ohio school systems.

Nazis Appear at First Board Meeting

At my first official board meeting in July, 25 young men dressed in Nazi uniforms filled the front row seats in the administration building's auditorium at a regular monthly school board meeting.

Their uniforms were complete, from black boots to swastikas on their arm bands and Nazi flags flying. Behind them were girls in uniform, known as Brownies. To my surprise, behind them were their parents and supporters. I felt sorry for these young men; they didn't know what it meant to be a Nazi. The public wasn't allowed to speak at these official board meetings. There were public hearings on all items before the board, at which individuals could speak. But this was not allowed at regular board meetings. The Nazis were there to make a statement. This new superintendent would have to deal with them if he attempted to educate black children.

This wasn't the last time I would see the Nazis. I placed a policy statement before the board, which was known as a Statement on Education and Human Rights. The board was hesitant to adopt this statement since they felt that the state of Wisconsin was very liberal and never discriminated against anyone, and the school board was already on the right side of human rights. That's what they said to themselves. However, to accommodate the new superintendent, they said, "Why don't we hold a hearing on this statement? And that will be the only item on the agenda."

A meeting was called, and at this meeting many groups in the city testified that the board didn't need to adopt the statement because it was well known that Wisconsin and the school board believed in equal rights and it didn't have to be a part of board policy. Then the Nazis came forward. They had life-size figures of a Jewish stereotype and a representation of a black person in the appearance of a gorilla. Their presentation was that these two groups had not evolved enough to be educated, and it was a waste of money to try. Their presentation was terrible in every respect. But when they had finished, the other groups that had advised against the policy said they supported it, and the board should pass it so everyone knows what side they are on. At the next regular meeting of the school board, they passed the policy unanimously.

The John Birch Society Calls
the New Superintendent a Communist

Before the September meeting of the school board, the John Birch Society had delivered their latest newspaper to each board member's desk. The newspaper had a headline stating that the new superintendent was a communist. Their reasoning was that I was from Ohio, and that the state superintendent, whom they called, said that he knew me. They went on to state that the state superintendent was a communist since, when he was school superintendent in Akron, Ohio, he led several Fulbright teacher exchanges on a tour of Russia. Of course, this bit of research proved that I was a communist, and I had to answer to some board members, questioning me to determine whether I truly was a communist or not. The Birchers never were satisfied that I was not a communist. The John Birch Society members protested the integration efforts in every way they could.

School Board Action

Feeding Black Children a Hot Lunch

The school board took noble action to rehabilitate inner city schools that were nearly 100 years old. The school system took great pride in the physical condition of their schools. The schools were always well maintained, and the floors were always highly polished.

Over a number of years after WWII, the school system built 67 new schools in the outlying areas of Milwaukee. These schools had room for additional growth so there were classrooms available for the children who were displaced from their schools during the remodeling. The policy of the board was to make sure that the children, black and white, didn't mingle or have contact with each other. The program was called "Intact Busing," since the black children were transported in school buses with black teachers and were to arrive at the school to go to separate classrooms, sometimes in separate wings of the school, and should have no contact with the white children. Therefore, they didn't go to recess together or have any activities that involved both black and white students. At lunch time the black children were to return to their old school site and walk home for lunch, while the white children had a hot lunch in the school's cafeteria. At the trial before a federal judge, the judge asked the school board representative to "give me one good reason why these children couldn't eat a hot lunch." Realizing the severe cold weather and snow conditions in the city of Milwaukee, any caring person would realize that these children could have eaten a hot lunch separately so they wouldn't mingle with the white children. Therefore, he asked the board's spokesman why they couldn't have a hot lunch. The board spokesman replied that the board didn't want them getting used to hot lunches since they weren't going to have hot lunches in their newly remodeled school.

This policy was eventually rescinded by the school board and the children in the inner city were provided hot lunches in their newly remodeled schools.

Attitudes of Teachers

Teachers Strike During First Year of Integration Under Court Order

In spring 1977, the teachers' union opposed the integration effort. Actually, some teachers didn't want to teach black children, or teach alongside a black teacher. Individual teachers called my wife and told her to persuade me not to force the integration of the teaching staff. Our plan under the court order was to do it with volunteers if possible. Out of 6,000 teachers, we had to assign only 23 teachers to meet integration goals set by the court. However, some white teachers were very upset that they would have to teach alongside a black teacher who hadn't earned their way into a majority white school. So in that spring of 1977, the teachers' union went on strike to thwart the integration effort. They went on strike for several reasons. It became clear they wanted to set a record in Wisconsin of having the longest strike ever in the history of the state, which was 25 days. It also became clear that, since the strike took place in the spring of the school year, they wanted it to run until the end of the year, so there would be no matriculation of students to the coming school year—with no graduations, no promotions, and no choices for parents to volunteer for an integrated setting. Since the union was against the integration effort, 2,000 teachers showed up at the administration building with the sole purpose of erasing race from their personnel records. I was told that 50 city police showed up to prevent them from entering the administration building, which was successful without incident. Eventually the strike was settled after 26 days, and the integration effort proceeded.

In-service Days for Classroom Teachers

The state superintendent met with the union and assured them they would get paid for the days that they were on strike. She then came to visit me in my office to tell me that they were going to get paid, and I told her that we don't pay people to strike. That's all part of the level playing field. They don't work, and we don't pay them. Well, she thought that I was wrong, that teachers in Wisconsin always get paid for the days they are on strike. This time they did not get paid while on strike in Milwaukee. However, the special master employed by the court brokered a deal with the teachers union. They would have to attend 26 in-service education days over a period of three years, which would center on human and race relations and improving the education of city children.

At one of the first in-service sessions for elementary school teachers, the school district brought in the nation's most prominent spokesperson on how to improve reading skills. There were several hundred teachers in the audience and the introductory remarks were delivered by the general assistant superintendent, who was a well-respected black administrator with a sterling reputation over at least 25 years of service. While he was making appropriate remarks, some teachers in the audience were talking, darning socks, grading papers, reading magazines and newspapers. In other words, they were not paying attention as you would expect from your own students in the classroom. Before the expert on reading was introduced, I was motivated to lecture them on good classroom behavior. In front of this expert, I think they were embarrassed by how they had been behaving, and, after my short lecture, they stood and gave me a standing ovation. I learned later that the union had instructed them to get through these 26 days, and don't get involved. They were told not to take the in-service sessions seriously, that this was strictly a way for them to get the money they lost while on strike.

Two Teachers Promote Prejudice

The two special education teachers who had a printing press available to them published a bulletin displaying a cartoon with an image of a black person as a gorilla, with a derogatory caption. They sent an adolescent black boy, a special education student, to distribute the bulletin to other teachers and staff in the building, which they thought was a hilarious joke. When it came to my attention I did not see it as a joke, but as a statement of racial bias from two of our professional teaching staff. I wanted to fire them but the union defended them. The best I was able to get was several days of suspension and they were required to take courses at the university on race and human relations.

Attitudes of Officials

Meeting President Reagan

President Ronald Reagan commissioned a study for the Department of Education which issued a report entitled *A Nation at Risk*. He and the Secretary of Education were making the rounds to large metropolitan areas, challenging communities and educators to improve America's schools. A conference that centered on this report was held in the Minneapolis metropolitan area.

I was president of the Council of Great City Schools, an organization of the nation's largest urban public school systems. I made a presentation at the conference, representing the largest school systems in America. I offered two recommendations that centered on the needs of the cities: a Marshall Plan for city schools, and a GI bill for classroom teachers. President Reagan arrived and shook hands with all the platform speakers, so I had the chance to greet the President, who seemed larger than life. I think he was wearing a protective vest. He seemed very natural when speaking to the audience, which now included parents and students from the immediate high school. It was very hot in this gymnasium-type auditorium. He took off his coat and sat on a folding chair and made his presentation and took questions from the audience. I was very impressed with his demeanor.

As a follow-up to the *A Nation at Risk* report, President Reagan established the Excellent School Award and recognized schools of excellence throughout the United States. These schools were judged to be the best in the nation, and subsequently were presented Flags of Excellence by the President in the Rose Garden at the White House. Several schools in the Milwaukee Public Schools received these flags over a period of years.

Senator Moynihan Supports Magnet School Legislation

I was in Washington, DC as a witness before the Joint Congressional Committee on Civil Rights. I was there to support legislation that would fund magnet schools throughout America. Wisconsin's representative from Whitefish Bay and Shorewood, Representative James Sensenbrenner, interrupted the proceedings with a short statement, stating that I was a trouble maker in Milwaukee. During his presentation, Senator Moynihan came into the hearing and sat beside me and put his arm over my shoulder. He wanted to know about me, where I was from, in order to get acquainted with me. He assured me that he was supporting this legislation because there were several cities in New York state that wanted magnet schools, including Buffalo, whose superintendent was also sitting at the witness table. I was not able to hear the presentation from Wisconsin's representative, but the Buffalo school superintendent said that Sensenbrenner was like Alice in Wonderland, which I didn't understand, since I was relating to Senator Moynihan. I made my presentation and left. The legislation had to get clear sailing from this committee on civil rights. It was eventually passed and signed by the President. The entire delegation from Wisconsin supported the legislation.

My First Meeting with the Mayor

In spring 1976, after the federal judge ordered the Milwaukee public schools to desegregate beginning in the next school year, I met face-to-face with the mayor of the city of Milwaukee. He had already met with mayors of other cities and had made preparations to keep the city of Milwaukee safe during these years of integration. He had conferred with the mayor of Boston, who gave him background on the court case in Boston and the ensuing violence. The mayor wanted to make sure that this did not take place in Milwaukee, so had lined up hundreds of US marshals from the Department of Justice, and had assurances from the Governor of

Wisconsin that the National Guard would be available in order to keep order in the city. After he told me of his preparations, I began to explain to him that our approach was different from Boston, that the judge had ordered a voluntary transfer of students using educational incentives, and our approach would be a lot more peaceful since parents had chosen the schools they wanted their children to attend. We wouldn't have the resistance and the violent activity that was reported in Boston. I had sent staff members to Boston to observe how they were operating under federal court order, and they came back and reported to me that there were two systems operating in Boston. One system was the old guard that was resisting everything needed to implement the court order. Another system, well-staffed by the court, was working hard to implement the court order as best they could. They said the judge was even involved in ordering the equipment and supplies for the schools. The old guard tried in every way to thwart the implementation of the court order and just make it miserable. I told them that we were going to do everything we could to have a unified approach to implementing the federal court order. I expected everyone to give it support.

Conta Legislation

State Representative Conta, in the Wisconsin Legislature, proposed the law that would encourage the exchange of students—minority to majority, and majority to minority—in the city as well as the suburbs. The incentives were in terms of financing each student and providing transportation for this exchange. The legislation passed and was signed by Governor Lucey, who supported this effort. The Milwaukee Public Schools lost their case in federal court, and this program helped the school district meet the goals of the court in desegregating the schools. Before the legislation was passed, I got a call from the Milwaukee mayor, asking if he and the delegation from Milwaukee should support this legislation

Governor Lucey came to Milwaukee to sign a bus safety bill that required mirrors on the front of school buses, so the driver wouldn't accidentally run over a small child.

and what advantage it would be to the schools and the taxpayers. After explaining the effects of this law, he was very supportive, and almost within moments the legislation passed.

Meeting in Basement of the Bishop's Cathedral

It was necessary that I meet with Catholic parents on the south side of Milwaukee, since they sent their kindergarten through eighth grade children to Catholic schools, and had traditionally sent their high school children to public schools. Therefore, I needed to explain to them our plans for enrolling students in high schools, so they would have an equal opportunity, along with other parents, to enroll their children in the special programs that were now available to them. There may have been as many as 200 in the audience, as well as the Bishop and the Catholic Superintendent of Schools, and me on the small stage. There were short introductions and then I was introduced. Since it was a family gathering, I introduced my wife, who was in the audience. After my presentation, the meeting came to a close, and I asked the Bishop and the Catholic Superintendent which way they were going to leave the stage. I told them that I was going to pick up my wife, when at that moment I noticed that the Nazis had surrounded her. I don't know what they were saying to her, but she was very frightened. I went into the circle of Nazis and took her hand and we walked out of the room with some of the Nazis following us and clicking their heels close to our backs. I told my wife, "Don't give them any attention, and don't turn around. We're going to go straight to the car," which we did. The ones following us got into pickup trucks, and followed us for some distance. We then made our way home safely without any more confrontations. However, later on I was told that the young fathers of Catholic school children confronted the Nazis that stayed behind, and threw them out of the room. They were very upset with them.

The First Meeting with the City's Police Chief

Before the court order came down, I met with Milwaukee's police chief to tell him about the activities of the Nazis and other citizens attempting to keep black children from going to school. The Nazis were handing out leaflets that declared black children weren't fully developed and shouldn't be wasting their time going to school, and that they should go home. Also, along the route to school, black children were being sprayed with hoses by some residents who resented the fact that these children were walking by their residence on their way to school.

My first meeting with the police chief was unusual in several respects. I met with him in a room where he gave briefings to the policemen as they changed shifts. He was at least five feet above me with a railing between us, and I was in a position of looking up to him as if I were a school boy. He did listen to me, but made no response. I left with one of my staff members, both of us believing that the police chief had treated me poorly and he had more important problems to face than those that I had presented to him.

My second meeting with the police chief was after the court order had been issued. We met in his office around a small table. This setting was more to my liking since I could look him straight in the eye and tell him what we planned to do. I did relate the experience I had at the Bishops Cathedral, where I was confronted by the Nazis. He had now heard several stories from me about the Nazis, but on this occasion he told me he wasn't going to do anything about it. However, he did begin to do something about it because I saw in the evening local news that the Nazis were picked up for parking violations, underage drinking, and so forth. Finally, I never saw the Nazis again.

Bus Company Fails to Meet Contract

On the first day of school I visited several schools, which was my custom. I did it every year. On the first day of integration in September 1976, I discovered that parents were bringing their children to schools they had chosen by carpooling. I found that the buses arrived around 10:30. I called the office to see what was going on with this bus company. They were told by the spokespersons for the company that they ran their suburban routes first, and the city routes after that, believing that their experience in Boston alerted them to the fact that no one would board the bus. In Boston, the prior year, they had riots and parents were afraid to put their children on the bus. I believe we were in court the next day before the federal judge, complaining that this bus company had not met their obligations to deliver children on time to their schools of choice. The judge suspended their contract, and fined them $350,000, which was the total for the contract. This gave us the opportunity to go out and get another company or companies to provide transportation for these children, which we knew would come at a higher cost.

Governor's Commission

After the 43 specialty schools were in full operation, the governor established a commission to study these specialty schools, since there were many complaints about their excess cost, and the disparity between these schools and other schools in the city and state. After holding several hearings, the commission was ready to recommend the closing of the specialty schools in the city. However, a member of the commission said before we file this report with this recommendation, why don't we get some experts in here to support our recommendations? They felt they were safe in inviting two professors from Arizona State University, which is about as far away as you can get to find experts on urban education. After several days of study by these two experts, they reported to the commission, saying that, "Most school districts would give an eyetooth to have just one of these schools in their town or city. Why do you want to get rid of schools of this quality?" The report was paid for by the State Department of Education and came out of the state superintendent's budget. He complained to me that he never received a report, and didn't believe the governor had received a written report either. That was the end of that effort to highjack the voluntary integration of schools with educational incentives.

Governor Called a Racist

The Milwaukee Board of School Directors determined that the district had been segregated by acts of the state and the surrounding suburbs. The case now appeared before a different federal judge who had not heard the case against the Milwaukee Public Schools. At this trial, I was testifying through cross-examination by the defense attorneys, who quizzed me on the official acts of all the recent governors of the state of Wisconsin. They asked me about the present governor, and I testified that he supported a bill that would provide additional funds to school districts that developed minority schools. In other words, if a school moved from being integrated to becoming more minority in its student population, the school district would get additional funds. I just stated this as a known fact. In fact, there was additional testimony at the trial by another witness who pointed out this law that was proposed. The next morning, the headline in the local newspaper stated that I had called the governor a racist, and later that day he held a news conference stating that he was not a racist. Meanwhile, in court that morning, the reporters who were in the jury box jumped all over the reporter who wrote the story, saying that, "The superintendent did not call the governor a racist; he just related a fact."

Pacifying Black Legislators

Wisconsin was a very white state. On occasion there would be one black legislator. There was a tendency to pacify the one legislator. An example of this was the passing of a law that would allow for a voucher program for poor children in the city of Milwaukee. This program, of course, gave opportunities only to very few minority students, which meant that the large majority of these students were not covered by this law. Unfortunately, this law provided a pathway for private school children to receive state funded vouchers, which was eventually ruled by the Supreme Court to be constitutional.

Annual Meetings with Suburbs

The Chapter 220 law had provided for the transfer of students between the city and the suburbs, which required a structured meeting each year with each participating suburban school district. The first meeting of this kind at West Allis Administration building was very well structured by the school district's attorney and was conducted very peacefully, but ended in no agreement to transfer students. The second meeting the following year was in an auditorium with the committee members who represented both the Milwaukee Public Schools and the West Allis School District sitting on stage. The room was filled with West Allis residents who gave testimony that they would never send their children to the Milwaukee Public Schools because they were dirty, and poorly kept, and the children were undisciplined. After nearly 30 minutes of this type of testimony, a milkman who spent 25 years daily delivering milk to the Milwaukee Public Schools stood up and said, "All this testimony is lies." He went on to state that these were the cleanest schools that he had ever seen. The floors were highly polished, the children were wonderful, and were helpful each day in the delivery of milk to the classrooms. He never saw any violence in the schools. He was so authentic and convincing that not one word was said after that, and the meeting ended. But again, there was no agreement on the transfer of students from one school system to another under Chapter 220.

Attitudes of Organizations

Ten All-Black Schools Proposed

A very active black organization sent their representatives to my office with a proposal that we would develop ten schools in the inner city that would have only black leaders, black teachers, and black students. This effort on the part of the black organization would be operated over a ten year period. The purpose of this effort was to prove that if the school was organized in this way, in ten years it would be equal to any integrated school. In other words, blacks would be equal to whites. I told them that, under the court order, I certainly couldn't develop segregated schools, and there's no need to wait ten years to prove that blacks are equal to whites. They were equal now. They left disappointed that I wouldn't approve of their proposal, and they continued to criticize the integration efforts required by the federal court.

Making Rufus King High School the Finest in the State and in the Nation

I tried to visit all the schools, and my visit to Rufus King High School was very revealing. I saw students walking out of classrooms, gathering in the halls, walking out of the school, and sitting on porches of residents in the neighborhood. The residents I talked with were very perplexed that the school could not handle the student population and the police would not respond to their calls to remove students from their porches. Some even said that the students would walk straight through their houses on their way home from school. My answer to them was that this would all change, that I was determined to make this school, even though it's in the black neighborhood, one of the finest schools in America.

I was determined that the next school year we would have a brand new school program. I organized a committee of about 40 members of academia from the universities and private school authorities, as well as representatives from the Milwaukee Public Schools system. The charge of this committee was without any restraints: they were to design a model high school that would be their dream school, the most excellent school in the nation. They did not flinch from their charge and their commitment to serve the community.

Among their recommendations was that the curriculum should be organized around the International Baccalaureate. The students would be required to take four years of English, mathematics, social studies, and foreign language, and meet the state requirements for health and physical education. Students were to apply to attend this school knowing these requirements.

Understanding the nature of this school of excellence, teachers also had to apply for positions. The program was implemented in the next school year with children coming from all over the city and the suburbs to be a part of this school of excellence. At the end of the year, the students took the tests required by the International Baccalaureate organization and the results were sent to the headquarters in New York City. Since the scores they received from the first year of the program at Rufus King High School were so high, higher than any received before, the officials were very skeptical of the results. They thought they should come and carefully inspect the school to see if it was real. Happily, they were very satisfied that this school in the center of the black community had met all standards. It was my goal to provide excellence in education, but also to develop a school in which the black community could take a great deal of pride. I spent a number of nights visiting homes in the Rufus King High School community, and found that the residents were very supportive of this effort, and the marvelous change that had come to Rufus King High School.

In 1982, Rufus King High School applied to the federal Department of Education to participate in the Schools of Excellence program that President Reagan initiated as a response to the study *A Nation at Risk*. Two professors at the University of Wisconsin in Madison were hired by the Department of Education to evaluate the high schools in Wisconsin. They reviewed, of course, all the applications. In addition, before they came to Rufus King, they had visited a high school upstate which, over a period of years, they had helped to develop. They were convinced that this was the school they would be recommending to the Department of Education, but they had one more school they thought they should visit in the central city of Milwaukee. They felt they knew what they would find in this high school. But they were so impressed with the excellence displayed during their visits that they stated that, without question, this was the high school—Rufus King—they would recommend to be honored by President Reagan in the ceremony in the Rose Garden at the White House.

Rufus King Holds Assembly to Receive Flag of Excellence

A very special event occurred at Rufus King. Since the Department of Education thought that it was so special that an urban high school would be the most excellent in the state of Wisconsin, they sent out a Deputy Secretary of Education to present the Flag of Excellence to the entire student body at an assembly at Rufus King High School. It was a very exciting occasion with the pep band, cheerleaders, and various spokespersons celebrating this event. I asked the communications director, "Where is the press? Didn't you tell them about this very special occasion?" He said he sent notices out to all newspapers and radio and TV media. None of them appeared. They were all focusing on a protest by white parents who instructed their students to walk out of an assembly during a black history week if black students appeared on stage to make presentations in the program. The parents were assembled outside the high school, ready to receive their children, and they had invited the press to cover this protest. In the newspaper that night, there was a wide-lens photograph of television cameras and reporters, along with parents ready to receive the students. The priority of the press was to highlight a racial protest, rather than recognition of a high school that had received a Flag of Excellence from the President of the United States.

Large Manufacturing Companies Move Out of City to Find Skilled Workers

I was told a number of times by CEOs of large manufacturing firms that they could not hire our black graduates because they lacked the skills necessary for their employment. I challenged one company that I wanted to visit to see for myself what level of skill was necessary for manufacturing jobs in that firm. The personnel director took me around the assembly lines. One of the skilled jobs was to put a piece of sheet metal into a press, but a more highly skilled job was to put two formed pieces of metal into a press. I said, "I think our graduates could do that." In fact, the jobs were so repetitive they gave the workers rest periods and diverse tasks to reduce the risk of injuries.

I also called the personnel officer of the electric company because they had just advertised 45 openings for highly skilled workers. She told me they had thousands of applicants, and I asked her if they have skilled workers among these applicants. She said they had to make terrible choices between a highly skilled father and a newly trained son, both able to handle the skilled jobs that were available. So there was no shortage of skilled workers in Milwaukee.

It was never stated like this, but industries moving out of Milwaukee were looking for non-union workers and a guaranteed white population. One large company in particular explained at a conference they were going to Kentucky to find skilled workers. Now if you know anything about Kentucky, at that time it had very little technical education, and very poor public schools. So what did this relocation have going for it? Non-union workers and an all white population, and possibly some tax advantages. They didn't have me fooled!

Friday Night Services at Mount Sinai

In August 1976, I invited all the religious leaders and pastors to attend an assembly at one of the high school auditoriums, so I could explain the integration plans for the forthcoming school year, which was under court order. The Rabbi at one of the most prominent synagogues in the metropolitan area attended this assembly. He subsequently invited me to speak to his congregation at the regular Friday night services. He invited my wife and me to have dinner at their residence. I had a chance to review a scripture I thought I would use, which was in Isaiah. He said, "No, that's in Amos." I was glad to be corrected so I wouldn't make such an error before his learned congregation. However, they were very attentive in hearing my presentation. Afterwards, we went to the recreation hall, where they asked me numerous questions. Their interest was stimulated by the fact that we were exchanging students with the school districts in these suburban areas.

Not everyone in these suburbs was happy about the integration efforts, which was brought home to me when, on one Saturday morning, I visited a flower shop to buy supplies for my yard. As I was checking things out and paying my bill, a lady, all dressed elegantly with hat and high heels, as if she were going to Macy's department store to shop, confronted me. In other words, she did not look like a gardener. As soon as she saw me, she read me the riot act, saying that I should go back to the city where I belonged, and that I was not wanted in the suburbs and that I was a big trouble maker. The lady owner of the shop was shocked; I indicated to her that all was ok with me. I walked out quietly not responding to this verbal assault.

Speaker at AFL-CIO

At the monthly meeting of the AFL-CIO at Pulaski High School, I entered the crowded auditorium to witness the dynamic dialogue among union members and their leader. As soon as I was introduced, it became still as a church mouse. I was amazed that they gave me such rapt attention. I thought after this event that the reception I received was an indication that they had great respect for education and, at that moment, an educator. I gave them the background on the court case and how we were integrating our schools using educational incentives with volunteers as recruits. I had staff members ready to hand out literature on all the specialty schools and career specialties which we had developed, and told them they could study all the options and enroll their children for the finest schools. At a later date, the AFL-CIO officially endorsed the integration plans for the coming school year.

Senior Citizens Receive Fifty-Cent Hot Lunches at Elementary Schools

We had a policy at a number of our schools of serving senior citizens hot lunches at the noon hour, at a very low price of 50 cents. Some of these gatherings were operated like civic clubs with officers, regular members, and celebrations of holidays, birthdays, and the like. I visited a school where the seniors met in a small alcove just off of the main dining room, which served several hundred school children. They had nothing but praise for these school children, who were both black and white, as ordered by the federal court. They told many stories of how students related to them, bringing them their artwork, their creative writings, and helping them celebrate their birthdays. Now they wanted to talk about integration, and they said it was terrible. All it led to were fights, and violence, and schools should not be integrated. I asked them, "Where do you get this information?" They said, "From the New York Times, and television channels." I said, "Do you see fights here?" They said, "Oh no, these children are precious. They're wonderful." I replied, "Did you know this school was integrated?" That was a rhetorical question, which I left them to ponder.

Attitudes of Integration Efforts

Policies for Voluntary Integration with Educational Incentives

The federal court ruled in January of 1976 that the school district had been racially segregated, and must come up with a remedy. In preparation for this event, the board had approved three important policies.

The first one that was approved was called "High Schools Unlimited." Milwaukee Public Schools had fifteen high schools. This policy viewed these high schools as if they were all one large campus, and students could choose the programs in any one of these high schools, and enroll voluntarily. There were specialty high schools, such as Rufus King, which had the International Baccalaureate Program; West Division, which had the Fine Arts programs; Milwaukee Trade and Technical High School, which had outstanding programs in several skill areas. The other high schools had what they called career specialties, which would be attractive to students considering careers in areas such as the social service professions, medical, dental and health careers, solar energy, heating and air conditioning, agribusiness, and horticulture. Also, students could go to their neighborhood high school and then spend their afternoon in a skill center of their choice that was operating in another high school. We furnished transportation.

The next policy they considered was "Options for Learning." This applied to the elementary schools, which required that several specialty schools would be designed around the creative arts, gifted and talented, open education, ungraded education, bilingual education, language immersion schools, Montessori schools, individually guided education, computer school, math and science, and multi-unit schools. Parents would be able to choose which schools they wished their children to attend. They would go through a process of applying for these schools, hoping to get their first choice, but also could specify a second and third choice in order to satisfy their student's interest and educational needs.

The third policy brought before the board was called "Schools for the Transition." Traditionally, the schools had some eight-grade elementary schools, but mostly three year junior high schools. This organization also meant that the high schools generally had three grades-10, 11, and 12. This transition policy helped to reorganize so that the high schools would all be four year high schools, and

At Custer High School, we dedicated a new solar energy lab as part of the heating and air conditioning career specialty technology.

parents would have a choice of K-8 elementary schools, middle schools (6th, 7th, and 8th grades), and schools with only 7th and 8th grades. Eventually this policy resulted in a middle school organization, which was preferred. Some of these schools had specialty programs too, which made them attractive. Also, we knew that, over time, students coming out of the elementary specialties would want to continue their specialties into the middle school years, such as foreign language, math and science, gifted and talented, etc.

The Court Ordered Goals for the First Year of Integration Were to Have 53 Racially Balanced Schools

The Court also ordered that these goals should be met with volunteers. Since the school system had established these policies ahead of the court order, the plans went forward to sign up volunteers using educational incentives. Matching the choice of parents and students to the integration of schools was a formidable task. When it was all said and done, 67 schools were racially balanced and the first year goal had been met. The school system celebrated this event with a news conference that displayed all the names of the schools which were racially balanced. The city council president and the president of the school board were in attendance. Not everyone was completely happy with this accomplishment; in fact, an editorial said that the school superintendent and the board may have gone overboard in integrating the schools and are much too zealous. The next year, with intense planning, we were to racially balance 103 schools. When the results were in, we had, with volunteers, integrated 103 schools. Therefore, we didn't meet that same criticism with an editorial.

The Question of Busing

In all of these integration efforts there were more black children on buses than white children. This was thought to be a burden on black children, who were said, by some critics, to be forced to ride the bus. The critics viewed the bus ride as if it was the center of the federal court case. The court case, in fact, did not center on the bus ride, but on factors which would dismantle segregation. It wasn't equal bus ride, but equal educational opportunities. Following are several factors affecting the transfer of students.

The schools in the central city were tremendously overcrowded with, sometimes, the student population over twice the capacity of the school. Students were taught in store rooms, on auditorium stages, on gym floors divided with portable partitions, on playgrounds filled with portable classrooms, and, as the original court case stated, even in rented Sunday School rooms in order to confine the black population. In order to provide quality education to the central city schools, this overflow of student population had to attend basically white schools that had room for them. However, there were some critics who believed that an equal number of white students should have been assigned to these overcrowded schools, which I called the "equal suffering approach," where white children had to suffer the same consequences as black children from overcrowded schools. Of course, I thought these were cruel thoughts, since the children had nothing to do with the segregation that was found by the courts. It was the adults. We were trying to find some relief for the suffering.

For years, black parents had received information that gave them the perception that their schools were inferior to a majority of white schools. Therefore, given the freedom of signing their children up for these schools was an opportunity not to be passed up. They were willing to put their children on the buses to be transported to the schools of their choice. Also, black parents wanted the very best education for their children, so they were pleased that they had the freedom to select some of the finest schools in the city. Some of these specialty schools were at some distance from their homes, and so the children had to be transported to school.

The federal court order was not centered on providing equal bus rides for black and white children, but was to dismantle the segregation and provide integrated, quality education for all the children in the school district, both black and white.

Parents living in the central portion of the city have the same concerns that suburban and rural parents have for their children. That is, they feel good about putting their children on a school bus which provides comfort and safety, and assurances that they go and come from school under their watchful eye and that of school authorities. One of the most sensitive subjects brought before school boards when they look to cutting costs is the cutting of transportation. Parents will protest this over any other cuts suggested by board members and others. They want to keep the buses running above all else.

Also, it should be noted that, in Wisconsin, both private and parochial schools receive free transportation to schools at public expense. The bus ride for the city public school children is a privilege that these parents had enjoyed for a number of years, and, of course, would never give up the service provided by the local taxpayers.

In recent published articles, reviewing the court ordered integration in the Milwaukee Public Schools in the fall of 1976, it has been stated that black parents had been forced to send their children to white schools, but white parents had been given the opportunity to volunteer. It is an insult to believe that black parents are unable to volunteer their children and must be forced into school assignments. They are just as capable as white parents to make informed choices as to what is best for their children, when given the opportunity.

There were numerous opportunities for black parents to volunteer their children. Let's look at them, one at a time.

- They could volunteer to send their children to the suburban schools. Hundreds took this opportunity. None were forced.
- They could volunteer for newer and better-staffed outlying schools, which had more adequate facilities. Thousands took this opportunity, which they wish they had been available to them before. None were forced.
- They could volunteer to go to their neighborhood school where great improvements had taken place because of the integration efforts. The program was called Project Rise, which stands for "Rise to Individual Scholastic Excellence." (Incidentally, Project Rise received a national award recognizing their effort toward improving academic achievement.) Now there was room to provide special staff and services. Now the teaching staff could concentrate on student learning, rather than managing children in an

overcrowded situation. Thousands of parents participated in this effort, which involved them personally.
– They could send their children to private school and we furnished free bus service.

German School Bus Driver Quits

One morning the bus driver who transported black children to the German Immersion Language School came to my office and threw a paper down on the desk, saying that he quit. He was tired of driving a bus for these black children who only spoke German and he didn't know what they were hatching up behind his back.

Efforts to Deceive (the Milwaukee Magazine Article)

> "Oh what a tangled web we weave,
> when first we choose to deceive."
> **LORD ALFRED TENNYSON**

In the summer of 1986 I got a call from a reporter from Milwaukee Magazine requesting an opportunity to take a picture of children going to summer school. They thought that I was the instigator of the summer school classes for students that had fallen behind in reading and math and that I should be in the picture. We decided on Lee Elementary School, even though we had around 30,000 students in summer school.

The reporter and the photographer showed up and we gathered the children together for the picture. The children were very orderly and happy on this occasion and cooperated with the photographer and reporter. After a number of pictures were taken, the reporter asked the children to pretend that they were mad at being in school and to put on the ugliest face possible. They cooperated and several pictures were taken to get this scene just right.

When I got on a plane to Chicago later that summer, I found

the Milwaukee Magazine was on each seat with the picture of ugliness on the cover in full color and the article on the failure of the desegregation effort in Milwaukee as a feature.

So that is where the deceit began and continued throughout the article. The intent to deceive was extended with the techniques of journalism, such as selective quotes and misrepresentation of data. For example, the test results were displayed as if the school district was trying to deceive the public. It was, however, an effort on the part of the school district to understand more thoroughly the data that resulted from changing the Iowa Test of Basic Skills to a new edition with new norms. The company did the research to make comparisons from the old to the new test and the new test norms. We needed this type of research in order to make the comparisons to test results which we were monitoring year by year since we began integrating the schools.

Ironically, we had two University of Wisconsin-Milwaukee professors testify before the board that the Iowa Test was an easy test and gave better results than should be believed. I challenged that and said I would match our students against the university staff and we would see how easy this series of tests is. The university failed to respond to the challenge, but the Milwaukee Journal staff thought it was an interesting challenge. They brought the idea before the publisher; he thought about it and, after consultation, said that if their staff did poorly on these tests the public would never forget it and it would be a black mark against their entire company. Eventually the PTA leaders thought that some group should take up the challenge and they decided to get volunteers who would take the tests. Most, if not all of them, had some college education. The adults had slightly higher scores in reading and vocabulary and the student population at the high school level sharply excelled in math.

The article was thoroughly done but the intent from the very beginning was to deceive.

Attitudes in Athletic Events

Efforts of State Athletic Association to Isolate M.P.S. Athletes

A meeting was called by the Wisconsin Athletic Association that was structured around planned testimony from athletic directors in several of Wisconsin's school districts, stating that they no longer wanted to associate with the athletic programs of Milwaukee Public Schools (M.P.S.).

Their testimony included a statement that M.P.S. facilities were inferior to their facilities and were often in disrepair. Things such as holes in football fields, and rocks in baseball diamonds, and we didn't have swimming pools in all of our schools.

The next list of charges was that our athletes were inferior to theirs—that we gave them very poor competition, particularly in swimming and golf. In other words, they no longer wanted to associate with us and have us in their leagues or schedules. I think they would have been happy if we had just left the state.

After more than 40 minutes of this type of testimony, I stated to them that I had been an administrator in small town school districts and suburbs, and I knew from experience the nature of their upkeep of schools. Additionally, there was such a great contrast to this in Milwaukee that we had more than 60 skilled craftsmen in our maintenance department and that, if anything needed to be repaired, it could be fixed at a moment's notice. I never saw a leaky faucet in Milwaukee Public Schools, since we had a preventative maintenance program. The schools were clean and highly polished, and were known for their excellent upkeep. In fact, the maintenance staff offered to build an addition to one of our high schools since they had all the skills to do that, and I approved. Therefore I took exception to this highly orchestrated testimony.

Then I asked the two athletic directors, one was for girls, and the other was for boys, to tell how many state championships we had won over the last 18 months. As I recall, we had six state champi-

I was told integration would spoil our athletic program. However, Milwaukee Technical High School won the state boys basketball championship during the first year of integration. A week earlier, the Washington High School girls' basketball team won the state championship.

onships, and one was in girls swimming. After they had provided this information, I asked the large group assembled how many state championships they had. They had none. This tells you very convincingly about how competitive our athletes were, both boys and girls. The meeting ended without any more comment.

Business Leaders Want to Form a Large City League

Early on, when we began to talk about integration in the schools, I was told that, within the city, integration would ruin the athletic program. Of course, this wasn't true. There were various efforts to restructure things and a group of businessmen came to my office with a proposition to put before me. They had an agreement that we would form a league of large cities, such as Philadelphia, Cleveland, Chicago, Detroit, Milwaukee and Minneapolis. The high schools in these cities would form a league in which they would play each other, and no longer play schools within their state. They had worked out the finances so that we could use commercial jet airlines to transport our teams and our fans to these cities, and would I agree to join them in this proposition.

I told them, "Absolutely not. You've been hearing all this discussion about court ordered integration, and we're not going to follow the line of more isolation and segregation. We'd even be more deeply in trouble with the courts." Therefore, they left disappointed.

Washington High School Boys Basketball Champions

Often, when our teams entered the playing floor at the University of Wisconsin in Madison, they would receive a round of "boos" from opposing fans. Our fans never reciprocated, but it was obvious that there were negative feelings toward our teams, which often had a majority of minority students. Our Milwaukee coach recognized after the first game that his team members protested too much on the official calls. He told his team, in readiness for the championship game, that they could win against five, but not against eight, since the opposing team had five members and the officials numbered three members. If they played their game, and didn't protest and turn the officials against them, they could win the state championship. I observed at the beginning of the game that Washington High School basketball players were not protesting, but were overdoing it by telling the officials, "That was a good call," and gave them pats on the backside, which happens only in sports. The coach quickly called a timeout, and told his team that this was not what he had in mind. Instead, they should not react to anything; just play their best game, which they eventually won.

This team was booed as they took the floor in Madison, Wisconsin.

Girls Score Well in Loss

Riverside High School's basketball teams made it to the playoffs and now were scheduled to go to the state finals. The girls' sports were always downplayed in the local newspaper. In fact, for a long time, they never even carried the scores of their basketball teams. The girls would come to my house and go over the Saturday paper, disappointed that they were not even listed. A call was made to the sports editor, and we finally got the girls' scores placed in the newspaper. Then, we complained that they never wrote the girls' games up, as they did the boys' games, and that girls should be treated equally. Therefore, after this game with the Milwaukee suburb school, the headline was, "Whitefish Bay Girls Score Well in Loss." The girls that came to the house couldn't believe that the first article that appeared in the paper featured only suburban girl athletes, and nothing was said about the city athletes who won the game by at least 20 points. A call to the newspaper resulted in a response worse than the ignoring of city athletes, which was, "Our reporters live in the suburbs. They never go to a city game, so they don't know your girls, but know the girls on suburban teams. That's why the article featured them."

The girls wanted to know what was going on. They had tears of sadness but couldn't understand this type of treatment.

Two High Schools Take Championships in Track and Field

The boys' track and field team of a large south side school, South Division High School, won the state championship. To celebrate this, they held an assembly in a large new gymnasium which could accommodate an indoor track event. They had at least 40 members of their track team demonstrate their physical skills in the events they won, and they also showed off their muscular prowess. I was very impressed by this event, and now I went to a much smaller high school, Riverside High School, on the other side of town. I met the principal and we were on our way to the auditorium where they were holding their celebration. On entering the auditorium, I said, "Where is your team?" There were only four folding chairs on the stage. He said, "Well, they'll be sitting on the stage." I said, "Is that it?" He said, "Yes." Well, finally, four very slender girls appeared in dresses on stage and took the folding chairs with their legs crossed, and that was the championship team. They had to take every event in order to become champions, which is quite an achievement. I was amazed at the contrast between two championship teams, one boys and the other girls. Very seldom do two high schools in the same school district take championships the same year. However, the following year, both of our boys and girls teams took the championships at a single high school, Custer High School.

Threats on My Safety and Also on My Family's Safety

Several threats came through the mail from the White Citizens Council, the Nazis and the Ku Klux Klan. I immediately turned them over to the FBI. After receiving such threats, I thought that they had come to get me. Two robbers, believing the house was empty since my wife had gone to Florida to be with her very ill mother, broke into my house and came to my bedroom. I could see their silhouettes in the window since there was a storm that early morning. My first thought was that, "They've come to get me" and then I said, "Who's there?" I saw them turn and leave the bedroom. My daughter was in a nearby bedroom and I tiptoed into her bedroom to tell her there were robbers in the house and not to scream, and we were going to let them leave before we called the police. The police were called and came rapidly to my house, searched it thoroughly, and took fingerprints. Since the robbers were looking for money, they had touched a lot of cookie jars and other containers that they thought might have money. They did pick up my billfold, which was on the lamp stand in my bedroom. They had taken the money from it but had dropped it on the sidewalk. School children had picked it up and taken it to the nearby school. The principal called me and said he had my billfold. The police questioned me about having a gun. I told them, "I don't have any guns in the house." They thought I should since my life was being threatened. In fact, my son said the police often had unmarked cars on the street in front of the house, providing protection from time to time.

We had a third floor apartment where we gave housing to international students. The two female students who were there at this time were from Korea, and large burly policemen knocked strongly on their door early in the morning while they were sleeping. When they opened the door, it must have scared them to death, thinking back to their days in their own country when a knock on the door was not a comfortable feeling. We explained to them the reasons for the police being there, that it was a matter of protection.

I went off to work as usual, and my daughter called her mother in Florida to tell her about the robbers being in the house. She was in the kitchen, and at that moment she recognized that two knives were gone out of the knife rack. My wife, such a sweet person said, "Oh my. They might have hurt themselves, because Lee had just sharpened those knives." This was typical of her responses, always thinking of the other person's welfare.

Several months later the police apprehended the two robbers. They happened to be students at the University of Wisconsin at Madison, and had been engaged in several robberies in Milwaukee. While they were in the house, I recognized that they were on marijuana and the police confirmed that they were hooked on drugs.

In another instance, my office secretaries had been busy receiving daily phone calls, some of which were very threatening. They both came to my office one day with tears rolling down their cheeks, sobbing that, "You told us to let this go in one ear and out the other." With both hands they pointed to either side of their heads and said, "Some of it stays right here and makes us feel awfully bad. We can't take it anymore!"

Pictures Go Around the World

I was on my way to visit schools when I heard several sirens from police cars converging on one of our high schools. During the noon hour, our students were peacefully outside the school playing basketball and other games. A car full of white youths showed up, and got baseball bats out of the trunk of their car. They began beating up black students. The newspaper got ahold of this picture, which was sent around the world, showing how violent integration was in Milwaukee. I got letters from as far away as Australia, complaining about the terrible situation in Milwaukee. I never learned where these young men came from, but they may have, just on their own accord, decided at noontime to have a little adventure, and go out and beat up on some black boys in a city school. Apparently, they did come prepared with their baseball bats in the trunk. I believe the news media built this up as some major racial problem at the school, which wasn't true at all; it was outsiders beating up on students. It wasn't between students at the school.

Attitudes of the Business Community

In Milwaukee I was a member of the Rotary Club and several business groups. In fact, each of our high schools had a business partner, which was usually a major industrial firm, such as Briggs and Stratton.

Each month, I would be invited to a session, where an outside expert would give advice and counsel to the business community. Their advice was that production and manufacturing, such as was prominent in Milwaukee, should be replaced by service industries. I very quickly took exception to this approach, which would change the community from being very prosperous to becoming poor, because the service industry is related to bartering where one

The Superintendent, along with the business partner Waste Management, principal and teacher launch the trasnportation career specialty at Pulaski High School.

person trades his service in exchange for another's, but no wealth is produced.

From time to time, CEOs would tell me that they couldn't find skilled workers in Milwaukee. This argument would mean that they would have to move out of the city in order to find skilled workers. I took exception to this, also, so I challenged one manufacturing company to let me tour its industry. Their director of personnel took me on a tour. He also believed they couldn't find skilled workers, but at the first station I observed, a worker put a piece of sheet metal in a machine and it came out the other end, shaped. At the second station two pieces of shaped metal were put into a machine, which came out welded and looked like the form of a catalytic converter. I told him I thought our high school graduates could perform these tasks, that these are not highly skilled jobs. He told me that these jobs are so repetitive, that we have to break the habits of these individuals so they do not hurt themselves, by losing their attention to the task at hand. They go on breaks, or they do divergent jobs in order to stay alert. So I knew this charge of no highly skilled workers available for industry was unfounded.

Golda Meir School for the Gifted

The school board president wanted me to visit some of the schools before I ever decided to take the job as superintendent. He had me visit what was known as Fourth Street Elementary School, which was going to have to be torn down, because it needed so much repair, and had already been cited with polluting the downtown area from its coal-fired furnaces. After observing the school, I told him the school system ought to keep this building, because it was not spoiled by recent sub-standard additions. When we began our planning on integrating the schools, in some people's minds Fourth Street Elementary School became a desperate issue. No one would volunteer to send their child to that location in the city, which they thought was surrounded by drug dealers and the criminal population. So my answer to that was to make it a school for gifted elementary school children.

The first round we got 2,000 applications. This meant that we could fashion the school to fit the number of classrooms and have equal numbers of boys and girls and blacks and whites. So immediately it became an outstanding school. Over the summer we put in new windows, lighting, and a new heating system. In other words, we dressed up the school. Shortly after this, we had a petition before the board that we name the school the Golda Meir School for the Gifted. At the turn of the century, Golda Meir attended this school, beginning as a four-year-old through her elementary school years. In fact, when Golda Meir became Prime Minister of Israel and visited America, she went to Fourth Street School to visit the children. They called Golda Meir "Mrs. Shalom." So the headline in the paper was "Mrs. Shalom visits Fourth Street School."

Call the President!

We had made application to the U.S. Department of Education to receive magnet school funds, which amounted to several million dollars. We had several teachers under contract, and equipment and materials ordered. The applications hadn't been approved and school was starting within a day or so. I made several calls to Senator William Proxmire's office, who was a senior senator from Wisconsin. He had exhausted all of his contacts to assure me that we would have the money to support all these projects. Returning to my office, I said to the secretary, "We need to call the President of the United States." Without hesitation, she put a call in to the White House so I could talk to President Carter. I picked up the phone in my office and she had the President's Chief Domestic Policy Advisor, Stuart Eizenstat, on the line. I related my problem to him; he said, "I'll call you back." Within a few minutes I got a call, saying that the person in the Department of Education had 30 applications on his desk, and he was going through them one at a time. Our application had been pulled out and signed. Senator Proxmire's office would be given the announcement of the approval, and we would have our money in short order. Over a period of several years, we received as much as 45 million dollars of federal monies to support our integration efforts in the Milwaukee Public Schools.

Board Discussion of Bilingual Coordinator

In August 1975, at one of my first school board meetings, and in my first year as school superintendent, we received a grant to support bilingual education in the Milwaukee Public Schools. I had interviewed several highly qualified individuals to be the coordinator and took the best candidate as my hiring recommendation to the board. I didn't understand it fully, but there was a lot of resistance to this appointment. I learned later that the board had just turned down a Hispanic person as an appointee to fill a board vacancy. The board went on record that they didn't want any Hispanic on the board. The person I recommended, also Hispanic, was an outstanding prospect in the community. That was the backdrop, and caused a wide discussion of this appointee, which was a surprise to me. I told the board that, by law, I was responsible for recommending the most qualified candidate, and they could not fill the vacancy without my recommendation. My recommendation was passed on a split vote, which caused the newspaper to comment that I'd met my challenge with the school board.

Walnut Elementary School

The Walnut Elementary school had been closed, but in recent years it was opened up again to confine more of the black population to the inner city. I had told the staff that if I saw a school like that described in the hearings held before I arrived, I would close the school on the spot. I think they guided me away from some schools. Would you believe that one night this school burned down? So I reassigned those students to integrated schools.

A Visit by a State Legislator

Most state legislators had no understanding of urban education. Some complained continuously about the Milwaukee Public Schools. A legislator from upstate Wisconsin called me and complained vigorously about wasting money on the Milwaukee Public School children. At the schools in his small town, students scored on state tests better than the students in some of our schools. I was very courteous and offered to accompany him on a visit to some of our schools so he could observe on site what was taking place in our schools. The first visit was to an elementary school on the south side. It was a modern school with large pane glass windows. They had written "Welcome" to this legislator in 43 different languages, which were languages that were spoken in the homes of the school children who were enrolled there. Upon arrival, he observed these languages, which probably had at least four different alphabet forms. He was amazed! I asked him point blank, "Do you think these children will test the same as the children in your legislative district, since some of them just arrived this year from various countries around the world?"

Save North Division

North Division was and is a very special high school in Milwaukee. First of all, while I was there, we built a brand new North Division High School, which had an Olympic sized swimming pool, complete with viewing stands, two large gymnasiums, one that could sponsor an indoor track and field event, and a large auditorium that could hold a large 2,000 student population. The auditorium had computerized stage equipment, so that backdrops could be programmed ahead of time for theater and musicals. We also built twelve science labs, with the largest preparation rooms you could imagine, with old-fashioned equipment, as well as the most modern science equipment in storage.

More than one event took place before we finished the new North Division High School. A fine arts teacher had left the ceramic kiln on in her classroom, which started a fire on the third floor one night and burned out much of the roof. So the question was, should we reassign these students to another high school, so they could complete their education? My maintenance staff had different ideas. They were bound and determined to get the school back in top-notch condition within a week. It was a four-alarm fire, so the damage was extensive. But they replaced the roof, repaired all the classrooms, and completely repainted the entire school, which was damaged from smoke and water damage. They finished this within a week, so that students could continue to attend North Division High School and finish out the school year.

Also, we developed career specialties in each high school and reserved the most attractive specialty for the new North Division

High School. Adding to the wonderful science facilities, we developed a clinic which met the hospital specifications for a model hospital room and a freestanding dental clinic, with a dental chair, modeling a complete dental office. The career specialty at North Division High School was in medical, dental and health careers, and it was designed so that students from throughout the city could come on a daily or part-time basis and participate in this career specialty. The career opportunities in this specialty were enormous, and the employment opportunities are numerous even unto this day. It's unbelievable that some critics said that I was trying to make slaves out of black children with this specialty. The critic's minds were so limited; they thought the only job opportunities would be mopping floors, taking care of garbage or working in food service. They couldn't see beyond the menial tasks to the highly technical skills and professions which this career specialty represented. I was arranging partnerships for this career specialty with the excellent Milwaukee County Hospital, the Lutheran Hospital, and the Marquette University Dental School, along with Wisconsin's Medical School.

There was a campaign to save North Division as it was, and it had widespread support. The support came from the black community groups and politicians who wanted to please the black community by supporting an all-black high school. I believed at the time we could have gone to the federal court, presented our plan for North Division, and won our case. But it didn't seem to be worth it, since all the other high schools were integrated peacefully, and the entire voluntary approach would possibly have come unraveled.

I was very disappointed that we were not able to make North Division High School integrated and a pride to the community, as was Rufus King. My dream was to have Milwaukee's finest high schools located in the black community so they could be a point of great pride. But I was unable to get the kind of support I needed, with so much emphasis on saving North Division as it was. We were, however, able to install the laboratories and facilities for the career specialty in dental, medical and healthcare careers.

I recall an opportunity I had to meet the student body at an assembly at North Division High School to explain our overall plans for high school students, and particularly for North Division students. They were very much aware of the campaign to "save North Division," and of course had a sense of loyalty to this cause. But they were very polite and heard me out as to all the possibilities for their future.

I went over all the possibilities that were available to them under High Schools Unlimited. They could go to Rufus King High School, which had high standards for academics, including the International Baccalaureate Program. They could go to Milwaukee Tech High School to learn how to build airplanes, cars, and computers, construct homes, and become very skilled workers. I talked to them also about the career specialties in the other high schools, which included data processing, foreign languages such as Japanese, Russian, and Chinese. But they could also choose North Division, which had the finest career specialty, among the full array of specialties offered in the fifteen high schools. This was the dental, medical, and health career specialty, which provided great training opportunities and opened up the whole field of opportunities, which would always be there. I could see they had wide-eyed interest in all this world of opportunity. However, I could see that they could also be easily influenced into saving North Division High School as it was.

I had additional thoughts about improving the community in which the high school was located. I found that it was an uphill battle. First of all, I was able to talk the school staff in the industrial and home economics departments into fixing up the homes immediately adjacent to the high school, and provide assistance to the residents there.

I had a friend who was an architect who wanted to join me in improving the community. He agreed to survey the community free of charge. He joined me in the effort to upgrade the community by making a slide show showing the well-kept houses, which, when viewed together, looked like a nicely fashioned neighborhood in a small Midwestern town. Then he showed me the intermittent homes which had no yard care, and little maintenance on the house with, for example, porches rotting and leaning. We both felt with the help of the construction industry and with the school's participation, we could remake the entire neighborhood near the school. But when I called the city housing authority, they said it couldn't be done, even though I had the support of the trade unions. Their answer was, "Some people just like to live like this, and you can't change them."

In another project, I wanted to get rid of old stores and factories that were boarded up or had shattered windows. I couldn't get any help on that. Then across the street from the entrance to North Division High School was a neighborhood tavern, which had been there long before the school was built. I asked the city if we could move the tavern, but they replied that the law protects this tavern, even though recent law prohibits liquor sales within a block of any school. School authorities at North Division said that known prostitutes were parading in front of the tavern during daylight hours, and they wanted to know what I could do about that. I went to the Ministerial Association, comprised of ministers who had churches in that neighborhood, to see if they could help me. They studied the situation but decided they "couldn't touch it."

A Wide Gap in Understanding of Poverty

From time to time there were high level meetings held at the Wingspread Conference Center. This is a center dedicated by the Johnson Foundation to holding national and international conferences on current topics. I was invited to speak at a conference where I was questioned about the drop-out rate in Milwaukee, which had been reported in the newspaper as 50 percent. I told them that I was very disturbed by what I heard from the state as to how they assembled this kind of data. My first call was to the communications director of the Department of Education, who said they put out the information requested by the governor of Wisconsin. I said, "Well, how did you come up with fifty percent?" He said, "Your annual rate is 7.8 percent, which comes out in an annual report every year, and that could be rounded off to 10. Since there are four years in high school, four times ten is 40, and 40 was rounded off to 50." I immediately called the state superintendent and told him how they came up with the numbers, and why did you approve that? He said we wanted a round number that people wouldn't forget, and this will help all school districts, because we have a statewide problem with the dropout rate. So I explained this to the CEOs who were assembled at Wingspread. I stated that, in the last annual state report, we had 2,700 students in the category of "unknown." In other words, we couldn't account for them. The report included four-year-old kindergarten through the twelfth grade, not just a four-year high school. Those in the unknown category were students who had moved out of the city during the last 12 months, and hadn't identified themselves in a public school enrollment in another city or state. Therefore, they were unknown.

One of the CEOs said that I was making excuses, and that we should go out and find those students, that someone knows where they are. He explained that, "In our neighborhood, when they move to another city or position, they tell you a hundred times where they are going. So there's no reason to think you couldn't find out where they are going." I realized right away they had no understanding whatsoever of poverty, or of transient populations. So I told them that in order to find these unknown students, I would need the services of the FBI, the CIA, Immigration Services, and the local police. They, in many respects, intend to lose tracking identity. Even if they go to a new school, they won't tell where they came from, and they don't have to. They leave in the middle of the night because their family can't pay the rent or utilities, and want to be relieved of the threat of bill collectors, for health or other issues. In other words, these CEOs came from an environment which had no understanding of poverty and had no idea what we deal with in a major city.

Making Schools as Exciting as the Street

In Milwaukee County, the judges took turns in juvenile court. I could tell that a number of them despised the assignment. There was a lot of talk in the media about students dropping out of school and a judge made a comment that I was responsible. He said I should make schools as exciting as the street. I never knew what he really had in mind—prostitution, drug abuse, theft, drunkenness? Is that what he had in mind?

Farewell Colobration for Hank Aaron

The Milwaukee Brewers baseball team wanted a big farewell celebration for Hank Aaron and his wife, so a special ceremony was held at County Stadium before a major league baseball game. Bud Selig, who was commissioner of baseball until 2015 and was part owner of the Brewers, invited me to make presentations to Hank Aaron at this farewell ceremony. When I was introduced in front of nearly 30,000 fans, I heard some boo-ing. Some explained it was "Oooh," as if they were impressed that I was there. But I think there were a few people who disagreed with the integration efforts going on in the Milwaukee Public Schools.

I had three school children there, presenting their artwork to Hank Aaron and his wife: one each from the elementary, middle and high school levels. I have found over the years that these presentations of artwork become prized possessions of the recipients. I had met Hank Aaron on an earlier occasion. I was taken to the door of the locker room with my son in hand, and Hank came to

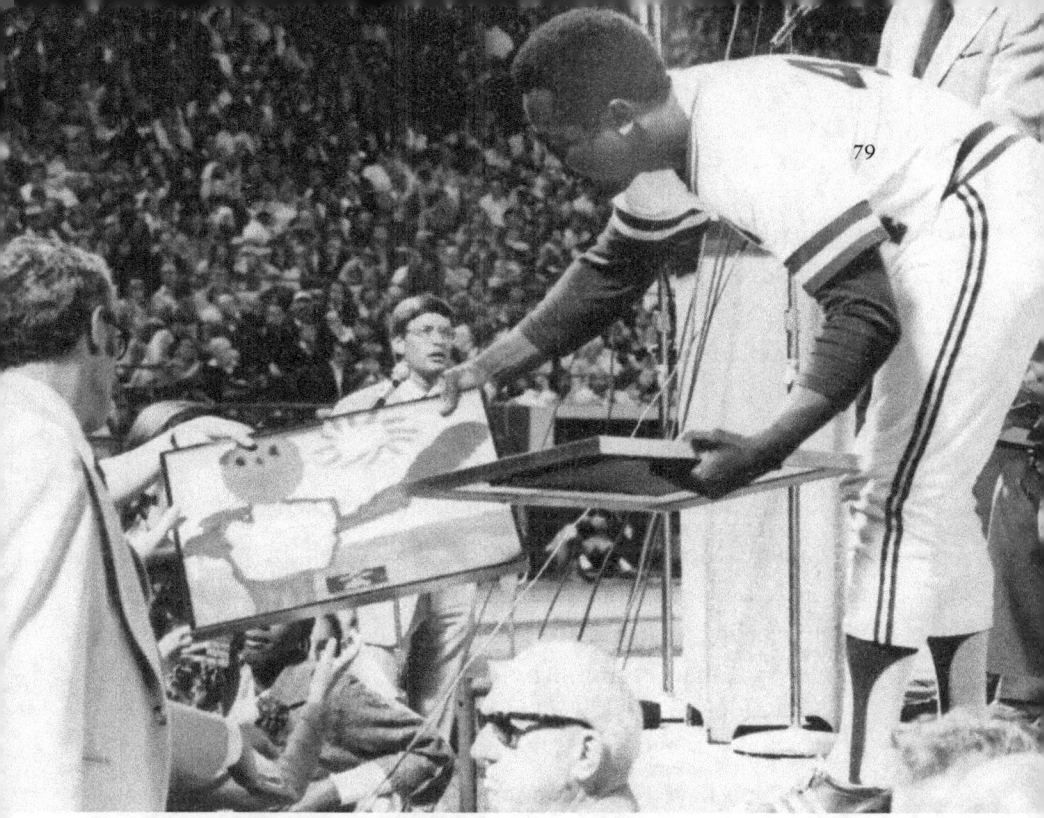

Bud Selig, part owner of the Milwaukee Brewers, invited the school superintendent to make a presentation at this ceremony honoring Hank Aaron. Three Milwaukee public school students presented their prize-winning art to Aaron and his wife.

the door, signed a baseball and gave it to my son. I was surprised at his stature. He was so tall, lean, and lanky. I expected someone stockier as a baseball player. I learned from one of Hank Aaron's best friends in Milwaukee that he received at least 100,000 hate letters as he approached Babe Ruth's home run record.

The war Between the French and German School Children

I got a call one day from the principal of our language immersion school, which had both a French and German program in separate wings of the building. She couldn't wait to tell me that a war was going on. We had had a tremendous new snowfall, and the children had built a Maginot Line on the playground. The French children were on one side, and the German children on the other side, each throwing snow balls at the other. Now how could that have happened? They must have known at least a little bit of history!

A Student's Tears at Montessori Specialty School

Many teachers among 6,000 felt free to call me personally and tell me classroom stories, knowing that I would be interested. A teacher of five-year old students at the new Montessori Specialty School said that, each morning, a five-year old would have tears. So she asked him, "Do you like the school?" "Yes." Do you like the teachers?" "Yes." "Do you like what we're doing here?" "Yes." "So why do you have tears each morning?" He said, "I'm so far away from my mother that I feel sad. I let a bit of sadness out each day."

Discouraged Central Staff

I read in the newspaper about students in surrounding school districts winning first place in an academic or extracurricular activity. So I asked the central staff if our students were competing and never winning, or if they even entered the contests. They said we don't enter any of these contests. Why would that be? Because we don't want the children to lose and, again, it would be a negative mark on our schools, because they are bound to lose. Right off, I said, "I don't believe it. You mean we have 100,000 children, and there's not one bright one out there anywhere? I'm sure we could win our share of prizes in a fair contest, so I want our staff to prepare them for these contests, and I want to see some winners." I informed the principals of this policy of entering contests, and we began to win them, one after another.

The most spectacular one that year was from our new career specialty in computer technology at Washington High School.

After the first year of the computer technology program at Washington High School, student Jason Bukvich entered a contest in New York City, won first prize and a $41,000 scholarship to MIT.

One of our students entered the contest, which was the first for this contest, and he went to New York City to participate. The test was not on data processing, but on how a computer is built and how you program this machine. He took first prize, and got a $41,000 scholarship to MIT! So it proved the point that if we entered the contests, and prepared the students for the material, we came off winners. In fact, Rufus King High School, which had the city-wide college preparatory program and featured the International Baccalaureate Program, entered the statewide Academic Olympics. They won several years in a row, so the authorities set a limit on how many consecutive years one school could win, to give others a chance. Otherwise, we would have won every year. They went on to nationals, and came in second place the first year they tried.

Through it all, and over a very short period of time, significant improvements were made in the schools, but not without opposition and a general feeling of hopelessness and negativity that had to be overcome. The next chapter describes the methods and techniques used to integrate the schools with volunteers, using educational incentives, which was eventually ordered by the federal court judge.

CHAPTER FOUR

A Case for a Voluntary Approach to Integration, Using Educational Incentives

"It is never too late to give up our prejudices."
HENRY DAVID THOREAU

The Setting

In the fall of 1975, Chicago attempted to integrate 400 children into all-white schools. These children were escorted by 400 city police in order to protect them individually from anticipated violence.

Also in the fall of 1975, Boston Public Schools were under a federal court order to integrate black and white students. The exchange of students was done in large numbers, but there was widespread violence. Some parents refused to put their children on school buses because they didn't feel that their children would be safe on the way to school or at their destination.

I sent members of my administrative staff to Boston to check things out, since we had received a court order to desegregate the Milwaukee Public schools in January 1976. In other words, we were under court order too. They reported to me that, in the central office of the Boston Public Schools, there were two highly dedicated staffs. One was dedicated to make sure the court order would not work. Another staff was working for the federal court judge to make sure the orders were followed. The federal judge was much involved in the administration of the schools, even to the point of ordering books and supplies for individual schools. The administrative staff was determined to make the integration effort miserable in every respect.

In 1975, the city of Louisville, Kentucky and the surrounding county were under a federal court order to integrate. In this case, they were dismantling segregation that was supported by law, until the Supreme Court reversed the "separate but equal" doctrine in the Brown vs. the Topeka, Kansas Board of Education case. An extensive change in students' school assignments was ordered by the court, and hundreds of children were assigned to racially balanced schools. Violence occurred immediately after school began, with people throwing themselves in front of school buses, as one example of protest.

There were many more examples of court ordered desegregation cases which didn't work very well, and which caused great disruption in the schools and in the communities that were involved. In any case, in desegregation, there are going to be critics and protests, so it seemed best to find ways to involve parents and students in the process, so they could join the effort to integrate the schools. There was every reason in the world to find a different approach. Keep in mind this is nearly 10 years after the U.S. Supreme Court ordered the dismantling of segregated schools.

I'm sure the federal judges conferred with one another on the best way to handle these cases, just as school superintendents checked with each other on how the desegregation was implemented. There was a sharing of information, as well as individuals posing as national experts on the subject, standing by to give advice and counsel to boards of education on how best to respond to the federal court orders.

It is now the winter of 1976, and the Milwaukee Public Schools are in federal court with an order to come in with a plan to integrate the schools. We set out to do that as quickly as possible, so that we could bring everyone along in the process and be ready to go back to the court with a plan to be adopted before school was out.

The first plan we put before the court was called "High Schools Unlimited." This had already been developed and approved by the school board. We used visual presentations to explain to the court how it would work to integrate 15 high schools. We first presented the vision viewing the 15 high schools as a college campus, where students had available to them all 15 high schools as opportunities for their education. Some city-wide high schools would have a specialty, which would include all the students enrolled. There were four of these high schools. One was already established, which was Milwaukee Technical High School. The other three were to be developed— one for business careers, another for the fine arts, and a very special academic high school for very rigorous college preparation. Each of the other high schools had one or more career specialties. These career specialties were developed by a committee commissioned to describe the career training which would prepare students for jobs beyond high school, or additional training in higher education.

The list the committee gave me was rather extensive, and included such career specialties as medical, dental and health, hospitality, international studies, including Chinese, Japanese and Russian, music composition conducting and theory, air-conditioning, heating and solar energy, data processing and office management, human and social services, computer technology, and transportation.

The second presentation to the court was "Options for Learning," which would be used to integrate the elementary schools. In order to fashion these schools, I went to a highly educated professional staff in the central office that had specialties in many areas of school curriculum. I asked the assistant superintendent to come in with a list of specialty schools that would be attractive to parents who would now have to make choices about the schools they wanted their children to attend. He initially came back with nothing, so I sketched out on a piece of paper some ideas that I had, and asked him to go back and develop these ideas with curriculum and instructional staff. I was waiting too long for a response, so I had him call a meeting of all the specialists. I outlined to them the approach we were going to use to integrate our elementary schools, using specialties, and that I was sure that in their professional training, they had visions of schools that monumentally support their area of the curriculum, such as language immersion schools, and schools for the arts.

I began to develop some enthusiasm among the curriculum specialists because I assumed they had some hopes and dreams for these specialized schools. I told them that I wanted their support in this effort by outlining those schools which would be the finest in the nation. They came back with a whole array of well documented schools and became ardent supporters of specialty schools, since they were of their expert creation. For example, if you were a French language specialist, the best school you could imagine would be having students begin as four-year-olds in a classroom where only French was spoken, and the curriculum through the grades would be French. Incidentally, our French immersion school was evaluated by a supervisor of French schools in Montreal, Canada. She was so impressed with our French immersion school that she told us our students were academically one year ahead of the French-Canadian students. Also, in testing these students on English tests, which were standard throughout the district, the achievement gap usually seen between black and white students no longer existed.

Each of these specialists had, over time, developed a realm of influence and support. The music specialists had acquaintances in the symphony orchestra, various choral groups, university staff, private teachers and tutors. Each of the curriculum specialists could dip into this environment of resources to gain support for their specialty school. This was tremendously important to their development, as well as to their continued existence. This kind of involvement wouldn't allow critics to close their schools, with this level of professional and academic support.

Also, there was a sequence of events put in place to fashion these schools and develop their vitality over time. In the immediate future we had to get them ready for the fall of 1976. But after we opened school in the fall, we began working on the coming school year with the new and revitalized specialty schools. In December we would bring the ideas before the school board. In January we would budget for these schools, and begin advertising, and in March, signing parents up for their choice of schools. Sometimes we would go several rounds in order to fill the schools. For instance, you might apply for a school that was over prescribed, so the second round you could get into your second choice, until you found a school with an opening.

The third presentation we made to the court was "Schools for the Transition." Traditionally, schools were fashioned after six-year elementary, three-year junior high and three-year high school design. In redesigning our schools under the court order, we desired to have four-year high schools, two- and three-year middle schools. Milwaukee already had an array of K-8 schools, so that school model would still be available to parents. It was designed so that the elementary specialty schools would continue into middle specialties, because the parents, once they start seeing the value of these specialties, want their children to continue, in most cases. The federal court judge, with a recommendation of the Special Master (who was appointed by the judge to assist him in the case) approved the voluntary approach, using educational incentives, to integrate the schools. The judge later established racial balance quotas to be met, and the number of schools to be integrated each year over a three year period.

Procedures and Techniques to Meet Court-Ordered Goals

1. Set specific goals with each school principal. They were to model their school; that is, they were to fashion their schools so they would have racial balance in each grade and class. If you had two first grades, you would fashion it so you had two third grades.
2. We set up three zones with racially balanced leagues within each zone, so there was a North, West, and South zone. (Lake Erie was in the East, hence no students) A specialty could be in multiples; one in each zone. Also the leagues were organized with co-captains, one black principal and one white principal. There were about eight to ten schools in each league.
3. These principals were to plan activities among the schools in the league, which would encourage the transfer of students. A number of schools planned picnics, fish fries, and outings for children in city parks, as well as tours of schools, so parents and teachers and children could get acquainted with each other.
4. The elementary principals had notebooks filled with information on the schools they were targeting for the children in their school attendance area. Parents were required to make choices and the principals needed to be well informed. One principal told me that he felt like a car salesman selling the prized schools!

5. The specialty schools developed brochures describing their school, which were attractively designed public relations tools. Also, individual schools, in order to make their schools look appealing, had attractive bulletins which they published from time to time when they had room at the school for new students.

The Historic Public Relations Effort: The Simulcast

I visited the largest and most prominent public relations firm in the city of Milwaukee. I approached the firm asking for help in selling the schools' integration program, with a budget of $10,000. The owners said that wouldn't even buy a sneeze here! In other words, we couldn't buy their services. They gave their services free of charge, joining in the effort to integrate the schools peacefully. The greatest contribution they made was organizing a simulcast one evening during the summer, which would help to sign up students to the school of their choice in the fall. All radio and television stations in the Milwaukee area carried the program, which originated on the stage of the Milwaukee Public Schools Auditorium. I personally interviewed several principals, who needed volunteers to fill their enrollment. Behind me were assembled 40 parents and teachers on telephones, taking the calls and signing up the callers. One of the principals had no volunteers at all yet for her school, which was located on Eighth Street in downtown Milwaukee. She had designed a model for sixth, seventh and eighth grade students. The school had no gym or cafeteria, but was located next door to the downtown YMCA. Students were to have swimming classes and games at the Y. On the first day of school, I made my first stop to see how things were going at the Eighth Street School. By some miracle, every seat was filled and the goals of the court were met.

I observed that the children were very happy to be in their new school. It was a miracle that took place that day, along with many others. The simulcast paid off!

Total Involvement of the School Community

In the spring, in preparation for planning for the new school year, the Milwaukee Public Schools had its own Simulcast, from its television station into every school auditorium throughout the city. Some people called this the Committee of 1000, because more than a thousand people were involved. The process I outlined to them was they were going to be involved one way or another in integrating the schools. First of all, they were to organize what became a welcoming committee, a committee at the school level, which would in turn send representatives to what was called a cluster committee. The cluster committee centered around a high school, and this cluster committee would eventually go to what was called the Committee of 100 meeting that would take place at West Division High School one evening.

The Committee of 100 met for the first time, with delegations from the clusters, with their table full of representatives and sign posts at each table, much like a political convention. So it was well organized, with several hundred in the bleachers observing the proceedings. They very quickly nominated and voted on co-chairmen, one black and one white. This was soon after the board president outlined the purpose of the Committee of 100 and stated the importance of participation in the process. Ten committees were organized that night that went to work on various aspects of integration.

I met with the Committee of 100 every month, sitting at a small table, spending hours answering questions and listening to many of their proposals. This was a very vital communication device

The Superintendent announces that the Milwaukee Public Schools, with their voluntary approach to integration, exceeded the court-ordered goals.

throughout these first years of integration. The dean of the college of education of Ohio State University, who was a friend of mine, and who also was an advocate of community involvement, was there as an observer that first night. He told me that he had never seen anything that worked so well, and which was so large and extensive.

These procedures set the foundation for the second year of integration, in which the federal court required 103 schools to be integrated. Again, we made the goal, to the credit of everyone in the school community, with 103 schools being racially balanced according to the court's racial quotas.

Everyone Helps Out on the First Day of Integration

I had a reporter ask to go with me on the first day of school. As we approached the schools, we found that there were welcoming committees for all the newcomers, with coffee and donuts, and juice for children. A number of volunteer parents and teachers were ready to register children for school. In many respects, these were very happy folks. In fact, we found in one school, at about 10:00 a.m., parents were bringing kids from the inner city to the south side school in vans. The school bus company had failed to pick up the children, and the parents were helping out with transportation to their new school. Many adjustments had to be made to make sure it all went smoothly.

CHAPTER 5

Leadership Style and Management Principles

*Management is too important to be left
to the managers.*

Throughout my experience as an educational administrator and my studies leading to a Ph.D. in educational administration, I learned to use leadership tools in order to get things done. The first two years of my career as school Superintendent of the Milwaukee Public Schools in 1975 and 1976 put those leadership styles and management principles to work in the face of an impending federal court order.

Anticipatory Management

When I arrived in June of 1975, there was great anticipation that the federal judge would rule on the case that had already been tried. Fortunately, I was given some time to help the school board and others get ready for the federal court's decision. An approach in which you help others affected by the decision to prepare for it is known as anticipatory management.

First, I wanted the board to adopt a Statement on Education and Human Rights. This was a policy statement that would guide the actions of the board and the school system now and in the future. Regardless of how the federal court ruled on this policy, it put the school system on the side of the law requiring that segregation be dismantled and encouraged the integration of the races.

This Statement of Education and Human Rights paved the way for procedures that would help to integrate the schools by using educational incentives, and encouraging parents and students to make choices. Several months before the January 1976 decision of the court, the Milwaukee Public Schools adopted three procedures which, when fully developed, would help to integrate the schools using educational incentives. These procedures covered all schools and grade levels. They were High Schools Unlimited, Options For Learning (elementary), and Schools For The Transition (middle school, K-8).

Participatory Management

The best way to be successful in bringing about change is to have those most affected participate in the process and development of the change. This is known as Participatory Management. In this case, the greatest illustration of this approach is the creation of the Committee of 100. It began at the school level at 167 schools with a simultaneous viewing of a closed circuit television presentation. They were briefed by the school superintendent on the court order and the role parents and others were going to play in developing the plans to be placed before the court. If approved, these plans would be implemented at the beginning of the next school year. Also, they were to elect representatives to attend a cluster meeting which would be held at each area high school. At this meeting, they would elect representatives to participate in the Committee of 100, which would meet at West Division High School. At the first meeting, the Committee of 100 promptly organized with co-chairmen and 10 sub-committees. They moved along with deliberate speed, knowing full well how important the deadlines were.

Keeping the School Board Informed

Keeping the school board informed was a formidable task. This wasn't easy since the school board had sides. There were eight conservatives and seven liberals or progressives. Board members were getting information from many different sources in the community and beyond. It was my policy to communicate fully to all board members; if one board member needed an answer, I communicated the answer to all 15 board members. I made sure they all got the same information from me.

Understanding the Change Process

Understanding how change takes place helps to get through this maze of change issues. For example, when a new idea is proposed, there are few that will adopt the idea. But, over time, others will join in supporting the new idea until there is a majority. There will always be holdouts who will never adopt the new idea or change. It is important to understand this. Otherwise it would be very discouraging to bring about change. This process of change was certainly evident in the integration of schools.

Manage by Walking Around

The need to know your schools and meeting the staff by walking around cannot be underestimated. As superintendent I, over time, had become acquainted with all 167 schools and their floor plans.

You can have some unique experiences by walking around. On one occasion, I was walking down the hall of a set of portable classrooms. The teachers came out of their rooms and asked me to walk softly because the books were falling off of the bookshelves. I already had very negative feelings about portable classrooms. This experience reinforced that. These were not appropriate for school children. They are something temporary, but they often stay long after they are useful.

On another occasion, as I was walking down the hall of an old school in need of repair, the ceiling plaster fell down, nearly hitting my head. The staff told me I should wear a hardhat when I visit old schools.

Walking around can give positive reinforcement to staff after observing their excellent performance and service to the school children.

You can inadvertently influence the staff to improve appearances. In this case, I mentioned that a portable on the school's playground made it look like a junkyard. The portable's siding, made of lightweight sheet metal, was bent and hammered and filled with graffiti. Later, when I again walked on this campus, this portable had been given a red brick veneer with new windows and doors. It reminded me of a one room school house common in rural areas throughout the Midwest. I would have preferred having it removed from the children's playground, but someone wanted to remove the appearance of a junkyard.

Feeding the Press

Keeping the press informed and communication open at all times was essential in making the case for a voluntary approach to integration using educational incentives. This approach was something new in the history of school integration. The print media in Milwaukee assigned two full-time reporters to cover the federal court case. However, on the first day of school in September 1976, I was told there were 45 reporters assigned to the schools to cover events throughout the city and the suburbs. There were no restrictions at all on these reporters; they followed their own leads and developed their stories as they were inclined.

I received a call on Friday afternoon from the principal of a large high school. He said there was going to be a story in the Sunday paper about "the Greasers" and their activities in his school. At this time there was a weekly television show that featured the kids next door with their high school classmates that were referred to as "the Greasers." The principal said that there were no Greasers in his school. This happened to be a setup by boys in the school who took advantage of a lady reporter who was posing as a teenage student. They fed her this story, which was featured in the Sunday paper. The very next week the principal called me and said that there would be another story in Sunday's paper; this would be a story of girl Greasers. There was no such thing as girl Greasers; the girls just wanted equal treatment. So much for feeding the press.

Generally the press was equally fair in telling their stories.

Sell the Product

The product was quality education for all school children. The means to this end was the process used to provide quality choices that would interest students and parents. Selling a court order is an uphill battle, but selling educational opportunities can be done with great enthusiasm and enormous energy.

Various tools and techniques were used to sell specific programs: The simulcast, word of mouth, brochures, appearances on radio and television, tours of schools, conferences, etc. Staying positive and optimistic is frustrating to some but contagious for many.

Meet All the Stakeholders

The superintendent must be willing to speak to all stakeholders, both large and small. Large groups would include the business community, labor unions, educational institutions, legislators, the media, parent/teacher associations, and religious organizations. You want to get their support and participation. There are also individuals who are very important in influencing public opinion. The obvious ones are the mayor, the city manager, the chief of police, aldermen or city council members, union leaders, executives at the chamber of commerce, and civil rights leaders. Others include community activists and individuals who are prominent in civic activities.

Listen to the Critics and Take Notes

It's important to listen to the critics. They are expressing thoughts that are circulating among some members of your community. Some are so extreme that you take note but you don't need to respond. These critics expose themselves and receive little if any support, such as, in Toledo and Milwaukee, the Nazis and the John Birch Society. Some criticisms need a response such as the brain drain (students going to the suburbs), the unsafe nature of school buses, the circulation of rumors, such as all black children carry weapons. Case in point: A TV station hired a young woman reporter from Chicago to stand with a camera at the entrance of a high school until she found a blonde girl to say she felt unsafe at the school because all the black students carried weapons. As soon as she had this recorded, she ran to the TV station and they played it over and over again. This sort of thing needs a quick response. You meet with the policy makers and challenge them for providing this type of reporting. They need to be confronted.

Don't let the critics distract you from your mission, although you can redefine your message.

Keep to Your Values

This list of values is somewhat limited. They stem from your childhood teachings from your parents and the guidance from others while you are growing to adulthood. You can't underestimate the influence of your education and the intellectual environment that surrounds you. In the face of all the reactions and decisions I had to make, I tried to stick to my values.

These were the most prominent values.
1. Respect others
2. Have integrity
3. Be generous with your time
4. Encourage peaceful resolution; reject violence in all forms
5. Obey the law

6. Accept and respect authority
7. Show kindness and forgiveness
8. Expect the best from others; give them the benefit of the doubt
9. Do what's right and just
10. Defend the weak and the poor

Plan with the Future in Focus

When you are working with the education of children and youth, you need to focus on the future. Therefore, we gave all the attention to opportunities and careers that will be there in their adult years. In 1976, we installed a solar energy lab and stocked a lab with 100 computers for teaching word processing. Some critics stated that no one had solar energy in Milwaukee, and that it was a waste of time and money to teach word processing since the offices in Milwaukee didn't even have electric typewriters.

Be Competitive and Display Your Best

When I arrived in Milwaukee in 1976, the central staff was so discouraged that they would not allow students and teachers to enter contests because it would bring shame to the district. I told them I didn't believe that and that we should have some very capable students in our enrollment of 100,000. I wanted them to prepare our students for competitive activities and that we would come home with the most prizes.

In the second year of integration, Washington High School's career specialty, computer technology, sponsored a student after his first year in the program in a contest in New York City. The student had to prove, through testing, his knowledge of how computers are made and their various components. He took first prize and received a $41,000 scholarship to MIT.

This started an avalanche of prizes that our students received each year over a number of years. Rufus King High School entered the State of Wisconsin Academic Decathlon and took first place for several years—until the state put a limit on the consecutive number of years an entrant could take first place.

After Riverside High School became Riverside University High School, students could take courses at University of Wisconsin at Milwaukee. UWM was the nearest neighbor to Riverside High School; therefore it was very convenient to establish this partnership. A student enrolled in an advanced mathematics course at the university. He learned of a math contest that the Wisconsin University System (which included 13 campuses throughout the state) was having for its math students, both undergraduate and graduate. He took first place on the test. It took several months to award the prize, since it was so unusual for a high school student to take first place in this array of competition. I learned about this award when it was announced at an awards assembly at the Riverside University High School. The University struggled with this decision but finally did the right thing.

Strive for Excellence

All the programs and specialties we developed were designed to be the best in America. Many were recognized by President Ronald Reagan in his program of Schools of Excellence and were presented flags of excellence in the White House Rose Garden. We even developed a program for the 20 lowest scoring elementary schools. These schools felt that they were left out of the campaign of excellence, so we developed a program called Rise to Scholastic Excellence, known as Project Rise. Their efforts to improve achievement received national recognition from a panel of educational researchers at a national convention.

Stick to Your Knitting – Be an Educator

Some management experts have recommended to a number of CEOs and their companies that they should stick to their knitting.

The chancellor of the University of Wisconsin-Milwaukee (UWM) and the Superintendent meet to confirm the partnership that converted Riverside High School to Riverside University High School. Riverside students then could take courses at UWM and earn college credits.

That means that they will be successful if they stick to what they know best and provide excellence in their product and services. Since schools are educational institutions, they do best when they stick to education and are headed by educators.

Have the Money

Bringing about meaningful change will cost money. Knowing where the money is and going after it is a fulltime job for your staff. The federal government appropriated funds to assist in the court ordered desegregation of schools. Major funds were allocated to the appellate court districts. Chicago, with its large population, was in our district. Since Chicago refused to desegregate, all the monies were available for the Milwaukee Public Schools. Adding to this, we assisted the federal government in passing the Magnet Schools Act. All in all, over a period of time, we received $43 million in federal funds to support our approach to integration using educational incentives.

The State of Wisconsin was also participating in the financing of the desegregation of schools with the Conta Plan, a school merger proposal. This plan provided state funds for the exchange of students between the city and the suburbs, and the integration of students within the city of Milwaukee.

CHAPTER SIX

Perspectives on Busing

"It's Not the Bus. It's Us."
REV. JESSE L. JACKSON SR.

Many different code words were part of the integration effort. One of the most prominent was the code word "busing." In my 43 year career in education, I had to deal with school buses and children transported to school by the yellow school bus. Also, I visited other countries that transported their children to what they considered the best schools. So I am presenting a perspective on busing which goes beyond the use of school buses to integrate the public schools.

The yellow school bus has been, and is yet today, a primary means of transportation of school children safely to school each day throughout America. It has become a vital and essential means of transportation that has proven very safe and dependable. If one is flying from coast to coast in America on a clear day, you would see these little yellow bugs taking over the countryside early in the morning and again early in the afternoon. Since the beginning of motorized transportation, the school bus has been an object of great interest since it carries precious cargo and because of the changes it has been able to support.

My experiences have given me the opportunity to view various perspectives on the subject of busing. The yellow school bus has been more than a means of transportation. It has also been an instrument to enhance educational opportunities, to consolidate resources, to bring American children from remote and isolated areas together and learn from a common experience and about each other, to promote a variety of school choices for parents and students, and to equalize the educational opportunities of children from diverse backgrounds.

Closing an Inadequate School and Busing Children into Small Village School

My first year of teaching was in a fifth grade classroom that was filled with an equal mixture of village children and children who were bused to school. The children who came on the bus were from an area in the county where a very inadequate school was closed. As always, there was some consternation. But the parents of the children who were bused were, on the whole, pleased with the newly assigned school that had indoor plumbing, hot school lunches, a school library and classrooms without mixed grades, which they did not have in the old school. Some of the children came from poverty-stricken areas where homes were made from scrap sheet metal and cardboard and had dirt floors. Some of these areas were referred to as "dog patch." In some neighborhoods, homes used a common pump and daily carried fresh water to their dwellings.

In the classroom we had very few problems working with these children; two of the brightest children in my class came on the bus. The parents and children raised very few questions about this situation of mixing. The ones who rode the bus were generally pleased to have a warm and safe ride on a yellow school bus to a better school.

First Administrative Position and Busing

I was principal of one school and supervised three other elementary schools in and around Letonia, Ohio in 1958. The superintendent and I were the only fulltime administrators in the school district. The school in which I served as principal had one school bus that came each day with a load of school children from the rural areas. The bus driver complained regularly that busing was a waste of money and rural schools were better than the village schools. He was the township trustee and was in charge of clean culverts, open roads in winter and the bridges on county roads. But now he was no longer responsible for schools. He told me that he actually tested the children that rode the bus to see if they were learning as much as they did in the "good ole days." The first graders he tested could only say the alphabet forward; in the "good ole days" they could say it forward and backward. He worried about the increase in taxes and the poor results the taxpayers were getting for their money.

Busing in a Newly Consolidated School District

The new superintendent and I were hired as a team to help put a school district together that was somewhat in disarray after being consolidated. Up to this point, because of disunity and conflicts over consolidation, the district had not been able to pass a bond issue or operating levy, which they needed dearly. We were the only fulltime administrators in the central office. The new school district included a city, several villages, suburban developments just outside a major city and large expansive rural areas. This was a monumental challenge. As one might expect, the school district included a very diverse group of socioeconomic classes and cultures.

The school bus was not always appreciated since it represented the new consolidated school district. In one village that originally had a one-room school, the parents protested the presence of the new buses by not allowing their children to load. So, in this case, the buses did not represent a safe ride to school, but a threat to a way of life in the village. Through communication and compromise the protest was short-lived.

The transportation system for this large consolidated school district was very expansive and complicated. These conditions, along with the attitudes and values of some parents, posed an enormous problem. The plans for opening day of school were very carefully laid to make sure that there was a classroom for each child and a teacher for each classroom. Intricate bus routes were put in place and routes and schedules were communicated to each parent. On the first day of school, only about 70 percent of the children anticipated showed up for school. This continued for several days, which was alarming to the administrators after the large investment put into teachers and buses. There was a host of reasons for this:

1. Some parents hadn't gotten the word yet that school had begun
2. Some were not ready for school with shoes, clothing and school supplies
3. Some of the children missed their bus, and
4. Some drivers didn't make their routes on time or at all. It actually took several weeks to get all the children in school.

The effects of poverty were in evidence in almost all schools after consolidation. With overcrowded schools and a fast growing population, students were assigned where there was room for them. A principal called me after receiving a new population and said that I should come over and see what I had sent him. He said that the children bused to his school in the first grade didn't have a good tooth in their mouths and that the teeth had rotted off at the gums. I asked him if he had talked to the parents of these children and he said he had. They told him not to worry about it, that they would get a new set of teeth later on.

Concurrently, we worked to pass bond issues and levies and were able to open six new schools in one year. They were full when they opened. Some of these schools brought running water, sewers, and paved streets into the neighborhoods for the first time. So the schools were instruments of needed change and improvements in the environment for the children and their families.

Children Bused on New Metropolitan Buses

The superintendent and I were both new to the big city. This was a large urban center that had lost its public transportation. We were interested in staying out of federal court over de facto segregation. We implemented a policy for minority/majority transfers, but we had no transportation system. The city and county were interested in restoring public transportation through newly passed federal legislation. The school system joined them in this effort and a levy was passed to cover local costs. Now we had nearly empty new buses running routes throughout the metro area. This all took place during the school year. The routes and pickup points were all in place to serve the entire metropolitan area. We gave schedules to the parents and students, and information was posted on the bus stops. The mass transit system was alerted that this would all begin on a day certain so they could look after the safety and the convenience of the systems. On this day, thousands of school children, both private and public, were riding buses to school on public transportation. It worked without a hitch. We were all surprised. And this event, along with others, kept the school district out of federal court.

Busing for Desegregation of a Large Metropolitan Area

The large city school system was in federal court on a racial segregation complaint. The trial was over and the city was waiting for the verdict. As the new school superintendent, I tried to prepare the community for the outcome of this case and ready them for the future, regardless of the federal judge. Several important policy statements were passed by the board that would provide for the integration of the schools in the metro area, using educational incentives and asking for volunteers to participate. There was a statement on Education and Human Rights, and this was followed by policies that allowed students, with their parent's permission, to transfer to schools outside their attendance area. Specialized schools and programs would be established to make educated choices and guidelines were provided to enhance the integration of the schools by race.

Initiating Specialty Schools and Programs

It was a struggle to get the specialty schools defined and the programs outlined. The first attempt was made by asking the assistant superintendent for curriculum and instruction for a list of schools that were either in the literature or in the minds of his professional staff that would be so special that parents would want to send their children to these schools if given the opportunity.

Keep in mind that in the big city we had curriculum specialists with master's degrees and Ph.D.s that covered all subject areas. We probably had, by far, the finest curriculum staff in the state.

The assistant superintendent came back empty-handed, saying that the policy was to have all schools alike and with equal quality. On several occasions I had been told that, in this big city, there were good schools and better schools. The good schools were black and the better schools were white. So I wrote on a legal pad a list of special schools that came to mind, and told him that his staff should take these or create some of their own and describe them in some detail. That didn't work, so I went to the staff directly and described what I thought would motivate them to come up with some good ideas. I said that if they had the opportunity to develop a school or program that would advance the achievement of their curriculum area in significant ways, what would it look like? I told them that, at this particular moment in the history of education, they had the opportunity to do just that and I gave them a few examples. I could see that they were excited and their creativity and professional skills were released and could not be stopped. Almost to a person they would come to own these new specialty schools and programs and support the plans for integrating the schools.

Busing for Segregation and Unequal Education

In this metropolitan area, if children were to have equal access to these schools and programs, the yellow school bus would be needed and the mass transit system would have to be utilized. But it is well known that buses have not always been used to integrate student populations. In the South, by law, they accommodated a system of segregation. In a visit to a rural family in the deep South, I was able to observe the doctrine of separate but equal, which was established by the United States Supreme Court and implemented by state and local school systems. One morning a new yellow bus came by the farmhouse on a dirt road. It picked up only white students. Later, an old worn and noisy yellow bus came by, picking up only black children. I was interested in seeing the schools that these children were being bused to. So I was guided to the school for white children. It was new and organized on a large campus with separate brick buildings for the various grade levels and subject areas. It served all the white children in the school district. I was told that the black children also had a new school. I was guided down a dirt road past an old saw mill and, nestled among white pine trees, was the new school. It was built out of cement blocks and had a shiny galvanized tin roof. There was no paint either outside or inside the school. I looked in the windows and the classrooms were equipped with tables and chairs, which looked like an odd lot of used kitchen furniture. I asked why the great difference in the quality of schools for black and white children. It was explained to me that the black children didn't want to come to school and often didn't come to school every day, so why have a quality school for them. They wouldn't appreciate it anyway. It is obvious that separate was not always equal.

A Policy of Confinement and Separatism

In the large metropolitan area, the urban school system was in court for a number of reasons, one being the policies of keeping the black children isolated and confined to the central area of the city. This also reflected the policies of local governments and the housing and real estate business establishment. The school system had built 65 new schools in the growth area of the city, while the black children were basically confined to schools that were built in the late 1800's and early 1900's. The inner city schools were old and crowded. Every available space was used for classrooms. Storage rooms, stages and gymnasiums were converted to classrooms. Portables were placed on the playgrounds. Church basements and Sunday school rooms were rented. Old unworthy schools were put back into service during this growth period after World War II.

Black Children Denied a Hot Lunch

In order to upgrade the inner city schools, which was a noble thing to do, children were bused to outlying area schools. These were new schools that had space for the black children. During the hearings on the court case before the federal judge, it was explained that the buses picked up the children at their old school classroom, with their black teacher, and were bused to the new school. At the new school, they were assigned by classroom to separate rooms and were not to come in contact with the other children from the neighborhood. They had separate recess periods. They were bused back to their old school to walk home for lunch, while the neighborhood children had a hot lunch in their new school. The black children had to walk back to their school to board the buses for the afternoon session. At the court hearing, the judge asked why the children could not eat a hot lunch at the new school. The answer given by a school staff member in federal court was that the school system didn't want these children to get used to hot lunches, since they would not have a hot lunch program in their newly upgraded school. With the cold weather and hard winters in the Northern city, one can only imagine how miserable this was for these children and their teachers. When I told this to some school administrators in the South, they said that they administered segregated schools but they were not mean about it. That wasn't altogether true in the South but I could appreciate their sentiments.

Federal Court Orders Comprehensive Desegregation Plan

In the middle of the school year, the federal court judge ruled in favor of the plaintiffs, and ordered the school system to come into court with a plan that would address the findings of unconstitutional segregation and discrimination by race committed by the school system over the years. These acts had to be remedied since they had lingering effects, which were still observable in the school system and the community. The superintendent and staff went to work on a comprehensive plan that fit the complaints, but was also consistent with the new policies that the school board had recently adopted. The court was skeptical of a plan that purported to generate results with volunteers and educational incentives alone. This type of plan had not been successful elsewhere, but the court was willing to give it a try. The court ordered the plan with guidelines that required numerical goals to be achieved over a three-year period of time.

Busing is a Code Word with Negative Connotations

In this situation, the word "busing" no longer meant a safe ride to school in a yellow bus. The word was used to put a negative tone on the desegregation of schools and was embellished at times as "forced busing" and "court ordered busing." It had become, not only in this metro area a code word for mixing the races, but also a code word used daily in the press and conversations of individuals and official bodies of government throughout the nation as a way of highlighting the miseries, hazards and protests associated with desegregation. The school system and the entire community had to go to work selling the plan and overcoming the negative reactions, which were very hostile toward busing. It was obvious that the buses would have to be used to overcome some of the effects of congregative acts on the part of many official bodies of government—but in this case the city school system. It is unfortunate that the yellow bus, which was necessary to facilitate the desegregation of the schools, would be viewed by many as a threat to the status quo.

The Mayor is Helpful

I knew the mayor would be very concerned about the potential fallout of busing, so I quickly scheduled a meeting with him in his office. The mayors of major cities met on a regular basis, and this mayor was a leader among them. Mayors shared their stories on busing and social unrest; therefore, he was well informed on the subject of busing as experienced in other cities. He gave me a resume of what he was already prepared to do to keep the peace. He had called the justice department and received assurances they would send a thousand marshals, if needed, to protect the children and to put down unrest. He also had assurances from the governor that the National Guard would be called up, if needed, to establish checkpoints and patrols in the city so that it would not be destroyed. He was proud of the fact that this city had not experienced burning and destruction, which happened in many cities after the assassination of Martin Luther King Jr. The National Guard was called out in great force on that occasion.

I then had a chance to review the desegregation plan and told the mayor that I appreciated his concern and the preparations he had made, but I didn't think we needed all those forces in the city. However, I wanted the city officials and the police department to know what we were doing so we would not have any surprises. Keep in mind that this conversation took place during the time that Chicago was going to try to integrate 400 black children into all white schools and were going to assign more than 400 extra police to protect them. It is obvious that these concerns were real. I mentioned that, in our plan, we would have thousands of school children on yellow buses going to their new school assignments throughout the city when school began in the fall. The police needed to be alerted to the need to provide security and safety, which they did each year when school started. There would be more traffic and activity on the streets and around the schools. Hopefully it would all be purposeful and peaceful.

Several weeks later the mayor called to find out about a piece of legislation that would permit and provide the funds for minority children going to the suburbs and majority children coming to the city. Would this legislation help the city financially? I told him that the transfers would pay for tuition and transportation costs. Because the legislators wanted to cover these costs to the suburbs, it gave the city leverage to request fair treatment for the city. I told him that, included in the legislation, is financial support for the cost of transfers within the city, and this cost would be covered in the state school aid formula that would be an advantage to the city. This would help the city cover the cost of transportation and other expenses dealing with the court order. He said he was pleased to get this information because the school system could avoid raising property taxes, which he anticipated with some trepidation. The mayor made some key calls. Within a few hours the state assembly passed the bill and the governor, eventually, signed it into the law. In his own way, the mayor was very helpful throughout this process.

Black Parents Respond in Great Numbers Seeking Improved Education

The desegregation plan gave black children, with parent's permission, access to schools in the outlying areas in the city and into the suburbs. For many parents this was an exciting prospect—leaving an overcrowded school with limited services and educational facilities and going to a newer school, which was thought to be of greater quality, where there was room. They also knew that they would not be isolated in these schools, but would be treated like any other student entering the school and assigned to integrated classrooms. The move to a home in a middle class neighborhood still presented many obstacles and barriers to these families, but the desire to provide a better educational experience was now open to them with free transportation on a bus. Therefore, the volunteers were numerous and the commitment made by these parents, in turn, helped those children left behind. With a much-reduced student population, the school could restore essential services and more attention could be given the students in their care.

The question came up often as to why did more black children ride the yellow buses than white children. Shouldn't it be equal? To get a grip on this question, the story of the Berlin Wall may help. The Berlin Wall, which was built in 1961, was a physical barrier that divided a city. Again, separate was not equal. West Berlin was a vital and thriving city and East Berlin was barren, void of activity and deteriorating, with buildings bombed out during the war still in disrepair. The contrast was enormous. Of course, the situation in this city was not as severe as it was in Berlin, but the psychological and sociological phenomena were similar. When the Berlin Wall came down in November 1989, throngs of people from East Berlin flowed into West Berlin. Very few went into East Berlin from West Berlin, unless it was for curiosity or to find parents and relatives left behind the wall. No one asked why the numbers crossing the former barrier weren't equal or did any one suggest that the government require that the numbers be equal. Under this court order, in this city, making the numbers equal on the buses would have been absurd. The plaintiffs would have complained that they didn't mean to have one problem replace another. In other words, they didn't mean to have white children in overcrowded schools, which would give no relief to the black children in the school and still deprive them of essential services. However, some people did subscribe to the equal punishment theory. They thought that if black children suffered from a containment policy, now white children should suffer in equal fashion.

Some believed that riding a bus was a miserable experience and that children should bear the suffering equally. If someone had experience in the suburbs, they would find that the yellow bus was absolutely essential to having a safe and comfortable ride to school, and that this service was maintained at all costs. I was superintendent of schools in a suburb that had a pickup point for every child, even if they lived across the street from the school. The parents wanted to see from their picture window their girl or boy get safely on the bus and return the same way. They could rest assured, knowing their child would arrive at school safely and return at the end of the day being cared for by the school system. We even had separate kindergarten routes for children who had a full day at kindergarten. It was the policy that these children had to be delivered at the front door and the bus driver see a responsible person take them in. If not, the child was brought back to school and the family was to be called to come and pick up the child.

For the safety of the children, the yellow school bus was not only a privilege, but also a necessity to suburban life. Some parents in the city felt the same way. They could see their child on a warm and safe bus transported to school, and didn't worry about their child braving the winter streets. And for themselves, the bus alleviated the anxiety of not knowing whether or not a child arrived safely at school. In this respect, they were no different than suburban parents. They appreciated the bus ride.

Efforts Made to Improve the Circumstances and Reputation of Inner City Schools

Not in all cases, but in most cases, an effort was made to put the specialty school in older facilities in the central city. This was done for several reasons. In the court case, it was reported that individuals shunned the schools where black students were a majority because the school-community environment wasn't safe.

White teachers and some administrators voiced this opinion as to why they didn't work in these schools. To overcome this, we thought that we would put the most attractive and compelling schools in the central city. Also, it was thought that the central city needed schools that they could take great pride in. This pride would come from the realization that these schools were not only the best in the city, but also had reputations that went beyond the immediate community and were revered by experts as the best schools that educators can offer. The reputation of schools would change drastically, with some of the best schools located in the inner city, and these children would get the best education possible.

There are those who believe that schools can improve conditions in the immediate community. If the schools display quality in every regard, pressure can be applied to members of the community to spruce up their property and improve the living environment. Some of the schools in the inner city were to be discarded because their heating plants didn't meet new emission standards. Remodeling them and putting them back in service actually added to the number of black students who could attend schools in their immediate community. But under the court order and the new policies of the board, these schools had to be racially balanced. The specialty school idea helped provide quality-integrated schools in the inner city, with advantage for all students and added value and pride to the immediate community.

An Example of Pride and a Struggle for Excellence

An inner city high school that was nearly in complete chaos was redesigned and, within a year, became one of the finest schools in the state and the nation. On my initial visit to this school I found everything in disarray. Students were in the halls during class time, going from classroom to classroom. Students were in and out of the school, telling me that they didn't have classes to attend. I toured the neighborhood and found students were sitting on the porches. The residents told me they didn't know what to do with them. Students were even walking through their homes on their way home from school. They wished someone would do something about this situation.

When I returned to the central office the staff asked me what I thought of this school. I think I said it was like a sieve with students going through classrooms, halls, outside doors and through homes as if they are being sifted. Well, are you going to close this school? Yes, I answered, at the end of the year this school will be closed and we will begin now to plan the finest high school that can be designed. I had already announced to the staff that if I saw conditions in a school that were as bad as those described in the court case, I would close it on the spot and assign the students to another school. In this case we waited until the end of the school year.

A committee was organized to design this school, which included administrators of university and private schools and the most capable teachers and curriculum specialists we could recruit from the city and suburbs. The school was to become the High School for the College Bound.

I was invited to homes in the immediate community to share some of my hopes and dreams for the school and to gather their concerns and responses. As we talked, they became very excited about the prospects of having this type of school in their neighborhood. These were homeowners who were part of the growing middle class of black families. The program was described and the standards were laid out for teachers and students. The school was reconstituted by having both students and teachers apply for inclusion. The enrollment was racially balanced and attracted students from the entire metropolitan area. Some school board members in the surrounding school districts sent their children to this school.

This International Baccalaureate Program was at the core of this high school's curriculum. After the first year in the program, students had to take prescribed tests in all academic subjects. The tests were sent to New York City to be graded. The results seemed surprisingly high to headquarters staff. They had never seen results like this from a first year school. They came to visit the school to check things out before they approved the test results. They were very pleased with what they found and, after their inspection, they approved the results. Fortunately, the High School for the College Bound had met its first challenge and had passed with flying colors. The next year they entered the state's Academic Decathlon and took first place. They took first place in this contest over several years.

After the national study which was reported as *A Nation At Risk,* the President of the United States established a program to find and recognize the finest schools in America. Schools throughout the nation applied for this honor. The process to review and award these schools began at the state level. Two professors at the state university were selected to review the applications sent to them from the Department of Education. They were to make site visits to evaluate the high schools. The professors had worked as consultants with a high school in the north central part of the state over a number of years. This school was one of the applicants. On their site visit, they used the criteria they had to determine the level of excellence in this high school. This school was determined to be excellent in every way. Now they were to come to the big city to visit an inner city school. They had already come to a conclusion before they arrived to evaluate this school. They believed there was no way an inner city school could compete in this test of excellence. However, after a strict and thorough evaluation of the school, they said there was no comparison. The High School for the College Bound was by far the best they had evaluated, and it was an easy recommendation to make to the Department of Education. The High School for the College Bound won the honor. The principal, the school board president and I went to Washington, DC to receive the award from the President of the United States at the Rose Garden. The principal brought a flag of excellence back with him, which was displayed in the school for all to take great pride.

The governor of the state established a commission to evaluate the conditions in the big city schools. The commission had many concerns about the specialty schools. Some members of the commission believed that these were elite schools that should not be part of a public school system. It was also believed that too much money was spent on these schools, which raised the costs of education in the city and in the state, exposing the disparity of funds spent among schools. Recommendations were prepared to present to the governor. They included closing the High School for the College Bound and several of the specialty schools. Wisely, someone on the commission said that it would add credibility to their recommendations if they invited some experts on urban education to make their assessments and recommendations. Someone knew of two professors at Arizona State University who were experts with national reputations. So they came to the big city to help the commission with its study. After spending a number of days visiting schools, they reported their findings to the Governor's Commission. Their conclusion was simply this: There isn't an urban center in America that wouldn't give its eye teeth to have any one of these schools and you have several here in the city. So why do you want to close out the best schools?

The teachers union wanted to defend their teachers who were assigned to other schools. They filed a grievance to restore the teachers who were not chosen for the redesigned high school. They complained that the teachers were not processed for the assignments under the provisions of the contract. Many months later, an arbitrator ruled that the teachers could return to the school if they so choose. Most of the teachers were now nicely settled into their new assignments for a year or more and didn't want to return to the school. But six teachers decided to go back to the school. Five were absorbed into the faculty of the school; one was not given a classroom assignment, but was given an office space.

Results of the Comprehensive Plan 1976

After several months of planning, the new school year was underway. Children were being greeted at their new schools by welcoming committees of parents and teachers. The school system had met court ordered goals and guidelines. The number of schools to be desegregated was 53 and 67 met the racial makeup required by the court. Although there were glitches in the transportation system, most of the children made it to school on the first day. In some cases, if the buses didn't make it, parents made sure their children got to the school of their choice.

One bus company with national experience for busing in desegregation cases didn't perform on their contract this day. The school system went into federal court seeking relief. The next day a hearing was held and the company told the judge that they didn't run some of the routes because they knew parents would not put their children on the buses, so they were not needed. Also, they told the judge that they ran their suburban routes first, and then came to the city to run some of these routes. This, of course, made the children late for school; they said the parents wouldn't care. The judge voided the contract and ordered that this company give the school system $350,000, which was the total contract for the year. The school system scrambled to contract other companies, which at this moment would cost a lot more. But the judge made monies available. Meanwhile, parents and other interested parties pitched in and got these children to school on time until the services were provided. This company provided school bus services to a small city in the state. The superintendent of this school district, learning of our plight, told me that he was dissatisfied with the performance of this company because they could not get the students to school on time. The company representative told him that he should get used to it, because they will never run on time. He, for a number of reasons, could not get out of that year's contract, but he would not do business with them again.

An Endless Story on the Use of Transportation Vehicles

These perspectives and experiences on busing children to schools appear to be quite comprehensive, but are not complete. Every day, there are situations dealing with school buses that are just as compelling and interesting. Educators and others love to share them. I can see yellow school buses pass my window every day of the school year. I can see children load school buses in our neighborhood and ride to a school that is on our street since we are the nearest neighbors to the school. So school districts everywhere are looking after the safety and convenience of the children in their care.

"Subwaying" in Japan

In other countries that I have visited, school children ride city buses, trolleys, subways and trains to school. In Japan, I saw kindergarten children, identified with a red cap and a backpack with the school name and colors, riding unescorted on the subway on the third tier down. Some came from all over the region in Tokyo to attend a kindergarten just a short distance from the gates to the

University of Tokyo. Enrolling their child in this school was the parent's first step in seeing that their child progressed through the system to complete their education in the finest university in the country. This would almost guarantee a position in the Ministry of Finance or in a large corporation.

"Training" in Belgium

In Belgium I observed school children boarding trains from small villages and taking a long ride into the city to receive the best education, which was not possible in their small town or village. In the evening, I saw them get off the train with their teachers, who also lived outside the city.

"Jeeping" in Berlin, Germany

In Berlin, before the fall of the Berlin Wall in November 1989, some students came to the John F. Kennedy International High School in military jeeps through Checkpoint Charlie into West Berlin, flying the flags of their Eastern Bloc countries. High level officials from these countries wanted their children to have what they thought was the best education, even though West Berlin was on the other side of the Iron Curtain. The Berlin Wall was highly fortified and meant death to those who tried to cross without authorization.

Riding "Elevators" in Moscow

The public school superintendent in Moscow was so excited and proud to show visitors from America the English Language Immersion Elementary School which was housed in a multi-story building in downtown Moscow. To get to their classrooms, the students had to ride several stories on an elevator. They entertained their guests with English songs. Some of the visitors sang along with them when they sang Sunday School songs familiar to those who attended Baptist churches in their youth.

Electric "Training" in Switzerland

A couple from Switzerland moved into the neighborhood with twin girls ready for kindergarten. The policy of the school district included special bus routes for kindergarten students who had to be delivered to a person at the home in the afternoon. On one afternoon, the mother of the twins was painting a room on the second story of the new house and saw the bus, but didn't feel it was necessary to get off the ladder and go down stairs to welcome the twins home. The bus driver took the twins back to school and the parents were called to come and pick up their children, which was the policy. The mother was very upset with this procedure and told the principal that, in Switzerland, the twins got on an electric train in the morning and came home from the train depot on their own.

"Fish Boating"

In Alaska I visited the State Department of Education offices in Juneau. There was a large room filled with teachers at desks preparing lessons and grading papers for their students who resided on fishing boats and other crafts offshore in the Pacific Ocean. The lessons were delivered and picked up each day by Piper Cub planes that used a shagging device to hook the lessons and hoist them into the plane. New technology, such as online learning via the internet, has likely taken the place of this practice.

"Boating" in Indonesia

In Milwaukee, two students from Indonesia who were enrolled at the university lived in our home. They told us that, in their homeland, a multi-island country, children are transferred to their schools each day via boats, since quality schools are not available on all the small islands.

"Flying"

Children on a small island in Lake Erie were transported each day to the mainland via a three engine motor commercial plane built by the Ford Motor Company.

"Buggy Riding"

The Amish in the Midwestern states take their children to school in horse drawn buggies. This was also common in the early history of these states, when parents took their children to the one room school in horse drawn buggies.

"Integrating Arab and Jewish children in Jerusalem"

In Jerusalem, the deputy mayor planned new schools to enroll students from their segregated apartments into a common school. She believed this was the best way to develop a stable peace in the future among competing groups in this city. She said she knew it was controversial and that she may not be elected to this office again. The mayor's office in Israel is like the board of education in America and, in this city, the deputy mayor was in charge. She was not elected to another term.

On another visit to Israel, the Minister of Education announced at an international conference that there were 13 magnet schools designed after the specialty schools in this American school system. The Minister of Education, when he was superintendent of the Tel Aviv schools, came to Milwaukee and stayed in my home. After visiting the specialty schools, he returned to Israel with the inspiration to develop these schools in his own country.

So it isn't the means of transportation that causes the conversations and the protesting of the bus ride. It is as Rev. Jesse Jackson liked to spin a phrase saying, "It's not the bus, it's us."

School buses do have something to say about the feelings of parents and racial bias. Early one morning I was shaving, getting ready to go to work after a night of several meetings with community groups. I heard a noise outside on the street, and I asked my wife what it was all about. She said, "A gray Mercedes diesel bus is now transporting children who used to ride the yellow bus to private schools." Since the yellow bus had become such an object of controversy, private school parents didn't want to have anything to do with it. They began to pay for the grey diesel bus instead of being freely transported to their schools by way of the yellow bus.

CHAPTER SEVEN

Responses to the Stories from the Front Lines of Integration

"Now this is not the end. It is not even the beginning of the end. But it is, perhaps, the end of the beginning."
WINSTON CHURCHILL

It's anticipated that individuals will respond in different ways to the stories that are included in the previous chapters of this book. There will be those who see some of the stories as so outlandishly absurd as to be unbelievable. How could anyone do that to the children in their charge, such as not feeding black children and sending them out on the street toward home at noon in the dead of winter while the white children were given a hot lunch at their school? This just couldn't happen. Who could believe such a thing?

Others will read these stories and can relate to them and tell you stories of their own which were experienced during those times. There are those who will see that progress has been made. They believe also that times have changed and these stories could not happen today. Others reading these stories will realize that there is still a residue of prejudice that exists today, but is expressed in different forms and toward different groups.

It's obvious that school personnel both in the North and South took sides on the issue of integration, much like the general population—which would include churches, school boards, government officials, and social and civic organizations.

Most of all, these stories can serve as being educational to those who have grown up knowing very little about the struggles of the 1960's and 1970's. They will not only be informed of the attitudes of people during this historical period, but may be shocked by the overt prejudice displayed. It is hoped that everyone can find ways to learn important lessons from a crisis of this magnitude. The following are some of the lessons that can be learned from these experiences.

1. Highly educated professional educators can hold racial prejudices that show up in their actions and which can have harmful effects on the young ones in their charge.
2. It becomes obvious that you may not be able to change a person's prejudice, but you can try to control their overt actions.
3. Individuals and groups who are in positions of authority must be held to the highest standards of human rights and the legal standards that uphold them.
4. Faced with an all-consuming crisis, educational leaders can seize the opportunity to bring significant improvements in the education of children and youth.
5. Educational reforms and improvements can be achieved only one school at a time.
6. Giving students and parents quality choices is more effective in successful change than arbitrary assignments.
7. Bringing people and groups along over a period of time in the process of change will yield better results.
8. Opposition to integration can be overcome with persistence and adherence to basic human values, along with creative means of implementing them.
9. Bringing children together from diverse backgrounds is not altogether unique to some American school systems,

but is more universally believed to be beneficial to the educational development of the young than some would like to think.
10. Knowing that the financial support for the education of the young is not unlimited, it is necessary to consolidate resources to improve schools.
11. In order to improve the education of the young, bold initiatives are piloted for a few to bring advancement in education to the many.
12. Education cannot be uniformly the same for all children if the special needs, desires and dreams of students and parents are met.
13. Some parents will go to great lengths to make sure their children get the best education available.
14. There is enormous resistance to change and the unsettling of social mores.
15. The prejudice of individuals and groups toward various ethnic, racial and socioeconomic groups is unfortunately too prevalent.
16. The yellow school bus and other means of transportation have been used to segregate as well as integrate schools.
17. If injustices persist and inequalities are not addressed, relief will be sought at the highest court of justice.
18. If given the opportunity and resources, educators can provide excellence in education for the young.
19. If given the chance, students from urban school systems can excel in academic contests when given adequate preparation and encouragement.

Early in World War II, England had experienced numerous defeats and now had achieved a couple of victories. Winston Churchill, the prime minister, stated, "Now this is not the end. It is not even the beginning of the end. But it is, perhaps, the end of the beginning." He knew there were still many battles to be fought

The Superintendent, along with the president of the school board and president of the city council, announces that 103 schools were successfully integrated according to the federal court order.

in this struggle against the enemies of the free world.

Winston Churchill's famous statement is especially applicable to integration in the Milwaukee Public Schools. In Milwaukee in 1979, with the involvement of the total community, the Milwaukee Public Schools had achieved, in Phase 2, the court ordered racial quotas in 103 schools. This deserved a celebration. It was also a moment to meet with the plaintiffs' attorneys to work out a settlement. The school district was facing a diminishing and aging white population with fewer children, and a young and growing minority population with ever-increasing numbers of children. Looking at the demographic trends and statistics on the racial makeup of each school, it became clear to all parties to the case that proceeding with Phase 3 would upset the racial balance that had already been achieved. Phase 3 was the year we were to racially balance all schools within the quotas ordered by the court. This appeared to be impossible.

Therefore, the parties agreed to a settlement that was presented to the federal court judge. He reviewed the document and, in 1979, agreed that we had met the requirements of the court and no longer needed to be under the court's supervision. Now we were on our own to no longer segregate and to maintain as much integrated quality education as possible. So this was only the end of the beginning. The real struggle now was to maintain the integration and enrich the education of all the children in our care.

This last story is noteworthy. During the concentrated efforts of the school staff and community to meet the federal court order by using educational incentives, I was holding a meeting with my cabinet one morning in Milwaukee. They, in unison, informed me that all our efforts may be in vain, since the demographics in the future will be such that the Milwaukee Public Schools will be comprised of a majority of minority students. My quick response at that time was, "What's wrong with minority students in a city having the best schools in America that educators can create and support?" After all these years, I still feel that way.

Photo Directory

Page **Photo**

27 Example of segregated drinking fountains in the South, as shown in the Smithsonian Institution.

33 Superintendent Lee McMurrin directs a 400-member band at a May Day Music Festival in Milwaukee, Wisconsin.

42 Wisconsin Governor Lucey visits Superintendent McMurrin in Milwaukee to sign a bus safety bill.

55 Superintendent McMurrin participates in dedication of a new solar energy lab at Custer High School.

62 Milwaukee Technical High School basketball team celebrates state championship early in the integration process.

64 Washington High School's winning basketball team, which was booed when they took the floor.

69 Superintendent McMurrin, school officials and Waste Management launch the transportation career specialty at Pulaski High School.

79 Milwaukee students present prize-winning art to Hank Aaron and his wife.

81 Washington High School student Jason Bukvich won first prize in a computer technology contest in New York City, which included a scholarship to MIT.

91 Superintendent McMurrin announces that Milwaukee's public schools have exceeded the court-ordered integration goals.

101 The chancellor of the University of Wisconsin-Milwaukee meets with the Superintendent to confirm conversion of Riverside High School to Riverside University High School.

130 The Superintendent, school and community leaders, announce that 103 schools were successfully integrated, which met the court order.

APPENDIX 133

Appendix of Media Articles

Page   Article

134   "65 Schools Reach Goal for Integration" – In the second week of the 1976 school year, 65 Milwaukee schools met the court-ordered goal of 25 percent to 45 percent black enrollment.

136   "Integration Goes Smoothly" – An editorial states that the first phase of court ordered desegregation went smoothly on the first day of school.

137   "McMurrin Keeps on Smiling" – Superintendent McMurrin visits seven city schools and one suburban school the first day of voluntary integration.

138   "Area Leaders Gratified by Opening Day" – Community and government leaders, including Wisconsin Governor Lucey, express enthusiasm and optimism after a peaceful start to court ordered school integration.

140   "A Letter From McMurrin" – Superintendent McMurrin thanks the community for its commitment and hard work in implementing one of the nation's largest voluntary school integration plans.

141   "School Integration Needs Volunteers" – Editorial states that voluntary integration requires the cooperation of every parent with a child in school, and the opportunities for children are exciting.

142   "McMurrin Answers Integration Questions" – A suburban newspaper reports on a 1978 community meeting with Superintendent McMurrin, in which he answers questions about the status of the school integration plan.

145   "Suburban Students to Get 10% of Seats" – An informal agreement designated about 10% of the space available in Milwaukee's specialty schools.

147   Guest Editorial by Dr. McMurrin on TV Channel 6 – A review of the status of the court order.

147   Comment from WTMJ Television and WTMJ Radio – Commentary urging the community to make school volunteerism work.

148   "Pact OK'd To Transport City Pupils" – The Milwaukee School Board and the County Transit Board agree to provide bus services to support transfer of about 4,000 students who have voluntarily transferred to other schools.

149   "Desegregation Plan Working" – Editorial praises black parents who volunteered their children to attend other schools.

150   "School Board Fumbling Chance" – Editorial states that if the school board offers a watered-down version of the segregation plan, it is inviting the federal court to impose a plan of its own.

151   "McMurrin-Board Rift Evident" – School board members object to the McMurrin proposal, emphasizing a split between the board and Superintendent McMurrin.

152   "Governor Signs Integration Bill" – Wisconsin Governor Lucey signed into law a bill, also called the "Conta Plan," providing financial incentives to support voluntary school integration.

153   "Reynolds Oks Plan for School Integration" – In July 1976, the federal judge overseeing Milwaukee's school integration approves the plan approved by the Milwaukee school board, culminating a lengthy process.

Milwaukee Journal
September 15, 1976

65 Schools Reach Goal for Integration

By David I. Bednarek
of the Journal Staff

Sixty-five Milwaukee public schools have met the court ordered goal of 25% to 45% black enrollment, school officials announced Wednesday.

The number is 12 higher than the number ordered by the court for 1976 and just one less than the school system's own goal of 66.

On opening day last week, 54 schools – the required number – had met ther court ordered percentage.

Although the overall statistics indicated success, Supt. Lee R. McMurrin said 175 students at one of the alternative schools – McKinley – would be advised to go elsewhere. He said the school would not be closed but would not be used as intended this year because not enough students volunteered to attend it.

McMurrin did not say how the school would be used this year.

Other Inner City specialty schools, which have had trouble attracting white students, will be continued even though they are not desegregated.

These are Lloyd Street, which is about 50% black; Philipp, about 79% black, and Garfield, about 67% black. McMurrin said he expected Lloyd to reach the court ordered percentage within a couple weeks and the other two later in the year.

Total enrollment reached 107,221 earlier this week, slightly less than had been expected before the desegregation plan was announced. Of the total, 36.5% are black. Last year, 34.3% of the students were black.

The increase in the black percentage follows the trend set in recent years, although school officials had hoped to stabilize the percentage earlier this year.

No White Flight

McMurrin said the enrollment figures indicated that there was no evidence of white flight. "Both black and white parents continue to send their children to the Milwaukee public schools," McMurrin said.

In the grade schools, the percentage of black students is 40.2%, considerably less than the 50% expected by some observers earlier. In the junior high schools the black percentage is 36.1%, and in the senior high schools it is 29.5%.

McMurrin said other schools could reach the court ordered standard by Sept, 30, the date the school system must report

APPENDIX

to Federal Judge John W. Reynolds on desegregation for this year.

(Note: unable to retrieve line)... high schools that were close to the court goal, but that there would be no push to get students to transfer to meet the goal this year.

These schools are Hamilton, now 20% black; Riverside, 47% black, and Washington, 54% black.

McMurrin said these schools and some other grade schools would be relatively easy to desegregate by next year, when the school system must desegregate another third of its 158 schools.

The only senior high school considered desegregated now is Custer, which is 29% black. There are seven junior high schools considered desegregated and 57 grade schools.

Here's the List

The grade schools now considered desegregated and their percentage of black students are: Bartlett, 35; Blaine, 31; Browning, 27' Bruce, 34; Bryant, 30; Burbank, 31; Cass, 30; Clement, 27; Congress, 40; Craig, 36; 81st Street, 34; 82nd Street, 35; Emerson, 35.

Engleburg, 25; 55th Street, 34; Fourth Street, 39; Fratney, 37; Gaenslen, 36; Goodrich, 26; Grantosa, 29; Greenfield, 28; Hampton, 28; Happy HIll, 38; Hawley, 30; Hawthorne, 27; Humboldt Park, 26; Jefferson, 39; Kilbourn, 30; Kilmer, 28; Kluge, 30; Lancaster, 31; Maple Tree, 30.

Maryland, 33; Morgandale, 29; Neeskara, 28; 95th Street, 34; Parkview, 33; Pierce, 40; Riley, 28; Sherman, 27; 65th Street, 31; 67th Street, 36; Story, 29; 38th Street, 42; 35th Street, 38; 31st Street, 38; 37th Street, 31' Thoreau, 26; Townsend, 36.

Trowbridgem 26; 27th Street, 41; Victory, 29; Warnimont, 29; Whitman, 28; Wisconsin Avenue, 36; and Grandview, 36.

The junior high schools considered desegregated are: Eighth Street, 31; Morse, 30; Muir, 31; Robinson, 43; Steuben, 38; Webster, 35; Wright, 36.

The Milwaukee Journal by JOURNAL CO., *Reproduced with permission of* JOURNAL CO., *in the format Republish in a book via Copyright Clearance Center.*

Milwaukee Journal
September 8, 1976

Integration Goes Smoothly

Milwaukeeans justifiably can feel proud that the first phase of court ordered desegregation, despite some inexcusable busing delays, began Tuesday without the senseless disruption that has occurred in some other communities. Indeed, the smooth implementation is powerful evidence that a significant desegregation plan might have been implemented years ago in Milwaukee, avoiding any need for a court order, had the School Board been willing to try.

Those who are inclined toward the gloomy view will point out that this first phase of the three year plan was the easiest because many schools happened already to be desegregated. Desegregating another third of the schools next year will, no doubt, be harder, since the parents most willing to volunteer their children for transfers presumably did so this year.

Nevertheless, this first step was significant. More than one-third of the schools now meet the court's definition of desegregation. Nearly half of the remaining schools, while falling short of that definition, have significantly more integration this year than ever before. Thousands of children will, for the first time, go to a school daily with many children of a different race. Thus the door to a better racial understanding in the next generation is opened.

If the educators work hard to make this year's integrated education meaningful – particularly in specialty schools that will have to attract substantial numbers of whites next year – then there should be thousands more participate voluntarily in integration next year.

At least equally significant this year has been the token racial exchange of pupils between city and suburb, with 350 Milwaukee minority children enrolled in half of the county's school districts. And two dozen suburban whites have taken advantage of some unique Milwaukee educational offerings by transferring into city schools this year. While this program, under a new state law, cannot yet be declared a full success, this first year's exchange suggests the possibility of significant city-suburban integration in the future.

When fully implemented, desegregation of Milwaukee Public Schools should remove, finally, a smoldering issue that has clouded far too much of the School Board's thinking for the past 15 years. With equal educational opportunity possible, attention then can focus on the crucial task of achieving quality education for all.

Therein lies a major strength of the Milwaukee desegregation plan, for it envisions widespread educational reform. Tuesday's first step into citywide desegregation therefore represents a significant step also toward making Milwaukee schools an educational anchor of stability in the community instead of one more reason for urban instability.

The Milwaukee Journal by JOURNAL CO., *Reproduced with permission of* JOURNAL CO., *in the format Republish in a book via Copyright Clearance Center.*

Milwaukee Sentinel
September 8, 1976

McMurrin Keeps on Smiling

By Rick Janka

School Supt. Lee R. McMurrin began Milwaukee's first day of school desegregation Tuesday with french toast and his usual smile. He ended it over coffee at a Marc's Big Boy Restaurant with that same smile – something few school superintendents in the country have been able to do after their first day of desegregation.

McMurrin bounced around to seven city schools, one of the system's satellite centers at Memorial Center and a Shorewood elementary school that had accepted 22 of Milwaukee's minority youngsters on transfer.

Never in McMurrin's visits or during his more informal conversations in the car as he drove from school to school did a single tinge of pessimism come from his mouth.

Instead he used phrases like "this is a miracle," or "this is beautiful" or "doggone it, this was hard work but it's paying off."

"There's no tensions anywhere, only friendliness," McMurrin commented as he finished the tour.

Standing in the parking lot of Memorial Center on the lakefront, the superintendent pointed to Milwaukee's skyline and said "all of these people out there – the businessmen, merchants, City Hall, everyone – will benefit from what we've started so well today."

While there were many problems Tuesday with buses being late or lost, McMurrin shrugged those off as expected with promises that they will be remedied as school gets further into the year.

The only problems McMurrin encountered were personal ones.

He couldn't find Trowbridge Elementary School on the South Side and had to ask for directions from several pupils waiting for a late school bus.

He almost locked his keys in the car as he hurried to a live television interview at Lloyd Street School.

He almost ran out of gas and had to quickly pull into a self-serve station and get a quick $5 worth.

He used his new car telephone for the first time and had to hang up on his secretary because he was making a left hand turn from the right lane of a four lane road.

In the schools, however, he found smiling faces to match his own.

"A year ago many people were saying we couldn't do this," McMurrin said. "Now we're doing it and the next two years of this are going to be smoother because of this success. Success will breed success."

McMurrin, who is seldom at a loss for words when it comes to discussing the Milwaukee desegregation plan, found himself somewhat speechless after his tour.

"I really just don't know how to express myself about all of this," he said. "I'm just so pleased, so pleased."

The Milwaukee Sentinel by JOURNAL CO., *Reproduced with permission of* JOURNAL CO., *in the format Republish in a book via Copyright Clearance Center.*

Milwaukee Sentinel
September 8, 1976

Area Leaders Gratified by Opening Day

By Louis Liebovich

Community and government leaders expressed enthusiasm after Milwaukee's first day of court ordered school integration passed peacefully Tuesday.

"I'm very optimistic about how things are going to work out," Gov. Lucey said in Madison. "It's really a credit to the leadership of Milwaukee. I think it may work out that Milwaukee will become a model for the rest of the country."

Mayor Maier, campaigning Tuesday in Raleigh, N.C., for presidential candidate Jimmy Carter, declined to answer questions about Milwaukee's first day of school.

County Executive O'Donnell in Milwaukee also declined comment.

School board members were especially happy Tuesday night.

"We did our homework," said board member Leon Todd enthusiastically.

"Thank God (it went well)," said board member Lois Riley.

Board member Thomas Brennan warned: "I didn't expect trouble. The trouble will come next September, because then you'll have large numbers of South Siders going to the North Side."

Gronouski Optimistic

Special Master John Gronouski, interviewed Tuesday at his Austin (Tex.) office, said he was very optimistic after hearing of Milwaukee's first day of school.

"Last January it was a shock," Gronouski said of Federal Judge John Reynolds' desegregation order, "but in the last few months I sensed a stabilizing of attitudes.

"Time will tell if this spirit of involvement will continue."

John Gilligan, an aide to Gronouski, toured six Milwaukee schools Tuesday.

Later he said, "My overall impression was that the people most centrally involved in integration – the teacher and students – are finally getting involved.

"Up till now it has been the courts, the board and the administration. I talked with teachers, who are very impressed with the big challenges before them."

Still Apprehensive

Lloyd A. Barbee, one of the attorneys for the plaintiffs in the school desegregation case, said that things appeared to be smooth and quiet but noted that most of the students being transferred were black.

"When the whites are assigned to good schools that are in the predominantly black area, I hope the reactions are equally smooth," Barbee said.

"I would always expect white Milwaukeeans to practice the law and order they preach to blacks. Since the court has ordered the board and administration to desegregate, the citizens and police should be prepared to obey the order or suffer the consequences," Barbee said.

Irvin B. Charne, another attorney in the case, described Tuesday as an historic occasion.

Surprisingly Smooth

"I did not think it would come off this smoothly," he added. "I recognize that school desegregation is only one step that must take place."

James Colter, executive secretary of the Milwaukee Teachers' Education Association, said the teachers were generally pleased with the first day.

He said the confusion over pupil transportation caused great concern among many teachers, but he said he hoped those problems will be resolved quickly.

Paul Baumann, executive director of the Administrators and Supervisors Council, said the principals and supervisors had a good first day.

"There have been many more work hours, but I would say the general attitude is that whatever is needed of them in this situation will be given," Baumann said.

Sees More Participation

Grant Waldo, co-chairman of the Committee of 100, said he had a favorable impression of the first day of integration.

"After the specialty schools are in operation, I think more white parents will become interested in having their children participate," he added.

Waldo also said he and Cecil Brown Jr., Committee of 100 co-chairman, will meet with Supt. Lee McMurrin late Wednesday afternoon to map out possible closer contact between the administration and the committee.

Community religious leaders greeted the the integration of the city's schools with a chorus of approval. For instance, Bishop Charles T. Gaskell, leader of the Milwaukee Episcopal Diocese, said Christians are pledged to integration because of the principle of equal opportunity and because integration is the law of the land.

Father John P. Hanley, archdiocesan superintendent of Catholic schools, will continue to work closely with public school officials to achieve integration.

The Milwaukee Sentinel by JOURNAL CO., Reproduced with permission of JOURNAL CO., in the format Republish in a book via Copyright Clearance Center.

Milwaukee Sentinel
September 7, 1976

A Letter From McMurrin

This letter from School Supt. Lee R. McMurrin was written at the request of The Milwaukee Sentinel.

Dear Milwaukee,

Today begins a new era in education here.

Our children are taking part in one of the nation's largest voluntary programs that combines quality education with racial and cultural exchanges.

This unique program will be monitored closely throughout the year not only by the Milwaukee community, but also by the rest of the nation.

We must continue to work hard to prove the value of this humane approach to educating our children in these complex times.

I join the Milwaukee School Board in thanking business, labor, industry, the teachers, the Committee of 100, the media and parent, community and religious groups for their commitment and hard work.

We especially thank and applaud those who volunteered to take part in this year's plan. However, we need more volunteers to step forward and help us.

The future of our schools and our city depends on this continued, enthusiastic commitment. We are counting on your support as we plan for the next two years.

Sincerely,
Lee R. McMurrin
Superintendent of Schools

The Milwaukee Sentinel by JOURNAL CO., *Reproduced with permission of* JOURNAL CO., *in the format Republish in a book via Copyright Clearance Center.*

Milwaukee Sentinel
August 17, 1976

School Integration Needs Volunteers

To anyone who watched or listened to Sunday night's radio and television simulcast on the progress of the voluntary school desegregation effort in Milwaukee, it was unmistakably clear that the people who run the Milwaukee School System are sincerely enthusiastic about the approach to integration being employed to satisfy a court finding that Milwaukee's schools are segregated.

It was also clear that much needs to be done to meet the interim goal calling for the desegregation of one-third of our city's schools by September. This is not to say that the accomplishments of the school administration to date have been unimpressive. Thirty-eight, or 58%, of the 66 schools targeted for desegregation by the administration now meet the racial ratio of the Federal Court. And 72% of the 53 schools targeted by the court for desegregation have been integrated.

Nevertheless, School Supt. Lee R. McMurrin concedes that "we still have room for many volunteers," especially for transfers to elementary specialty schools, where volunteer transfers are lagging.

Volunteerism cannot be lagging because of any failure by McMurrin or his staff. They have worked tirelessly to bring to Milwaukee a school system that would be unique and educationally sound, even without a court order. The prospects for education in Milwaukee are exciting, akin to a giant college campus where there is an opportunity for each student to progress at his own pace and acquire skills that might not be achieved in a traditional school setting.

But to make such a system work requires the cooperation of every parent with a child in school. Call it forced cooperation. Admittedly, that is what it is. It is forced volunteerism. The alternative is forced busing on a massive scale. The only difference, and it is not insignificant, is that the volunteer plan will be educationally beneficial to every child who participates. There is no educational benefit in forced busing. It only breeds animosity.

Therefore, the enthusiasm demonstrated by McMurrin and his aides is encouraging – far more encouraging than the attitude of the mayor of Milwaukee, who would rather dwell on the potential for violence than on the rewards of education; or of the county executive, who also did not participate in the simulcast, making the excuse that his children attended parochial, not public schools.

Leadership from City Hall and the County Courthouse on integration has been minimal. If the program is a success, the honor will belong to McMurrin, attorneys for both sides in the court fight, parents and even the school board. It will not belong to those who shirk their responsibilities.

The Milwaukee Sentinel by JOURNAL CO., Reproduced with permission of JOURNAL CO., in the format Republish in a book via Copyright Clearance Center.

Glendale (Wis.) Herald
March 16, 1978

I Think It's Just Great
McMurrin Answers Integration Questions

"We're going to be working this for a lifetime," Lee McMurrin, Superintendent of Milwaukee Public Schools, said of the voluntary integration program.

McMurrin's remarks were addressed to an audience of about 70 persons who attended the program on the Chapter 220 voluntary integration plan. The program was set up by Jim Landwehr, president of the Glen Hills PTA.

Under the Chapter 220 program, suburban schools receive state aid for providing spaces to Milwaukee students who want to attend those schools.

McMurrin prefaced his report on the voluntary integration program with a history on the events leading up to the filing of the 1963 Milwaukee school desegregation case. He traced the development of "separate but equal" laws in the south, saying that Plessy versus Ferguson was "a kind of blessing of the supreme court that led to a proliferation of such laws."

That case decided in 1896, declared constitutional a Louisiana law making it a criminal offense for anyone to occupy a seat on a train that was reserved for passengers of another race. But McMurrin also noted that the famous minority opinion by Justice Harlan foretold that separation of the races would cause racial strife and tension for 100 years.

"It has come true," McMurrin said.

McMurrin also recounted the story of a little girl in Topeka, Kansas, who was not allowed to go to a white school. The decision on Brown vs. the Board of Education in 1954, declared that separation was inherently unequal, which forced the southern schools to form a "unified" school system, McMurrin said.

"We, in the north, said this should have never been allowed to happen, we in the north never had laws like that," McMurrin said. "Nevertheless, during the 60s, we had racial tension. People who came here from the south felt they were back in the south."

In 1963, Lloyd Barbee, then president of the Wisconsin National Association for the Advancement of Colored People, filed a lawsuit alleging that Milwaukee public schools were, whether intentionally or not, segregated in reality.

"It took ten years to gather the evidence—and it took the judge two years to review the evidence. On Jan. 19, 1975, he found that Milwaukee schools separated students on the basis of race," McMurrin said.

McMurrin stressed that there were no rules or laws which enforced segregation, and attributed the separation of children in schools as a result of housing patterns and isolation. "But because Milwaukee is a law-abiding city, the school board began making remedies to assure children the freedom of access, a creative solution based on educational incentives. Many creative programs came out of that crisis," he said.

McMurrin reported on the success of specialty schools within Milwaukee and said that as Milwaukee approaches racial balance, many of these programs will be available for suburban transfer students.

Forms and pencils were provided to the audience for addressing questions to McMurrin. The questions asked showed concern for the cost and efficiency of the transportation, the possibility of a countywide school system, whether the voluntary integration program created lack of parent involvement, and behavior problems.

Transportation: "I rode a bus when I went to school. We had six kids in our family, and when we got on the bus, with our books, our lunchpails, and our musical instruments, the bus drive swore, right in front of my mother and father. We filled up half the bus and we were the first pickup.

"Milwaukee went from zero bus routes to 1,500 bus routes. When you have that many and do it on demand, you have problems.

We recently signed a contract with Eco-Tran and they say they can save us $2 million, and there is a time limit in the computer program for rides no longer than 30 to 40 minutes.

On the 1,500 routes picking up 20,000 kids, last week we had 17 infractions, such as a bus being late or missing kids. The problems aren't massive."

Countywide School System: "I hope not. I think we should keep educational decisions close to students and parents. Milwaukee's school system is large enough. I've said this from the day I arrived here, we can solve our problems with cooperation.

"It's the 12th largest school system in the country, but it's small town and that's how we try to approach things. We'd be twice as big if we were countywide."

Parent Involvement: "At the 4th St. school, students come from 90 districts, it's a downtown school, no one lives nearby. There they have 100% parent involvement.

"Other neighborhood schools are hard pressed to draw parents. What makes the difference? I think it's the parents' choice and commitment to a school."

Behavior and Discipline Problems: "We have to talk about our problems as well as our achievements. I know how it happens.

"Last year discipline problems involved white kids. The same number this year involve black kids. Our problems did not start yesterday,

"A black child is often followed with scrutiny, there's been negative research on minority groups all over the place. We just have to face up to it.

"Last year the Transport Co. drivers went on strike and this year the company tells us it's better than it's ever been. The behavior has improved because we cracked down. Just good hard discipline and I believe in it."

Could a Situation Similar to Boston Occur in Milwaukee?: "We could have gotten ourselves into a violent situation. We could have had a Boston, with police and the national guard protecting children from adult violence. But we tried to do it with educational incentives on a voluntary basis.

"There have been some angry souls but I'm proud of Milwaukee. We're a law-abiding city, we do believe in human rights, we're a good city, a friendly city."

How is the program working out for transfer students to the suburbs?: "The students feel good about their schools and that's the way it should be. I think it's just great. The children are making the adjustment, they're receiving tender care from the suburbs, the parents are satisfied with the program."

Jo Boucher, 1920 W. Woodbury la., has children at both Good Hope and Glen Hills schools and works as a volunteer at the schools. She said she had hope to learn more about the legal status of the Milwaukee school desegregation case.

About the transfer program in the Glen Hills school district, she said, "It has absolutely no effect on my kids. You just don't even know anything's going on."

She said that although her children

would probably remain in the Glen Hills district for college preparatory education, she thought that specialty schools, such as the medical and dental program in Milwaukee high schools, were a good idea.

Ray Rozek, 2001 W. Bernard la., is a teacher in the Milwaukee school system as well as the parent of a Glen Hills student. He said that busing has torn up the neighborhood shcool and that athletics and parent involvement suffer as a result.

He said it was difficult for students in the voluntary integration program to be involved in extracurricular activities. "The only way is to change housing patterns," he said.

Sue Dolinar, 4652 N. Elm Tree la., was typical of the well-informed and active parents attending the meeting. She said McMurrin had not said anything new, but that she supported the voluntary integration program.

"I don't think it's affected my kids at all, and that's good. Of course, at Parkway, 8% of our students are black anyway. What I was worried about is when the transfer kids went back home and realized they were disadvantaged, while other kids weren't. But I'm told this doesn't happen."

Ms. Dolinar is a volunteer teacher aide in the math program at Parkway school, and believes that the voluntary integration program has helped the transfer students academically. "I've seen it happen to 9 and 10 year olds. Some of the kids couldn't add and now they are doing division. They have no reason to goof around because they can do everything everyone else can do and as well as everyone else can do, and they feel good about themselves," she said.

Sigrid Peters, whose children attend Parkway and Glen Hills schools, and a teacher aide for reading classes, agreed. "I had a boy and you wouldn't believe he's the same boy. He'd do anything to please," she said.

Landwehr was disappointed with the low turn-out, however. Initially, he had scheduled McMurrin's talk for several months ago, but the event was canceled because of a snowstorm. Some parents at the table thought thought the turn-out may have been hurt because the Glendale common council also met Monday night.

Said Faye Miller: "I've never met McMurrin before. I've seen him on television. I'm impressed with the man."

Reprinted from Glendale Herald and used by permission of North Shore NOW.

Milwaukee Journal
August 6, 1976

Suburban Students to Get 10% of Seats

By Ralph D. Olive
of The Journal Staff

An informal agreement has designated about 10% of the space available in specialty schools in Milwaukee for suburban students.

David Bennett, new deputy superintendent of Milwaukee Public Schools, mentioned the 10% figure Thursday night at a meeting of the Committee of 100 in West Division High School. The committee is an advisory group to the Milwaukee School Board on desegregation matters.

Both Bennett and Supt. Lee R. McMurrin discussed the space set aside for suburban students after they were questioned by Jane Podemski of the Juneau Junior-Senior High School cluster. Mrs. Podemski said she was afraid the agreement with the suburbs would take seats from Milwaukee students.

McMurrin said the number of suburban students coming to Milwaukee in the fall would not be large, probably no more than 450.

"That might not be a large number in the overall picture, but it will be pretty large to the parents whose child cannot get into the specialty school because a suburbanite is sitting in the seat," Mrs. Podemski responded.

McMurrin also gave the Committee of 100 members a progress report on the school administration's efforts to obtain volunteers to transfer to help desegregation. McMurrin said he was confident that enough students would volunteer to make the program a success.

When asked if a lottery would be needed to assign students to schools outside their neighborhoods, McMurrin said:

"We believe our goals can be achieved voluntarily, and using this approach (a lottery) would be a last resort."

Ian Harris, a representative from the Lincoln Junior-Senior High School cluster, criticized the School Board's decision to continue the appeal of the Federal Court order to desegregate the schools. The 7th Circuit Court of Appeals in Chicago upheld the decision of District Judge John W. Reynolds, ordering the schools to desegregate. The board now has decided to continue the appeal.

Harris noted that the Committee of 100 had recommended the board not appeal Reynolds' decision. It seems useless to go on with a legal battle, he said.

"In the Lincoln cluster, we feel it is a waste of taxpayers' money," Harris said.

His statement was greeted with applause from cluster members.

McMurrin said the board was committed to the appeal as a matter of principle, but that in any case, the work begun for desegregation would continue.

The Committee of 100 passed a resolution asking the School Board to designate Spanish speaking students as an ethnic group and that plans for their role in desegregation be spelled out.

The motion was introduced by Aurora Weier, a representative from the Riverside High School cluster. Mrs. Weier said Spanish students were being ignored in desegregation planning.

Donald J. O'Connell, immediate past president of the School Board, spoke briefly and praised members of the Committee of 100 for their work.

"You have, I think, been an inspiration to the city," O'Connell said.

In another meeting Thursday, Bennett and Ruth Bishop, a curriculum specialist in the school system, spoke to parents in Townsend Street School, 3360 N. Sherman Blvd. The program was largely devoted to answering questions about specialty schools.

If an application to one school is rejected, parents will be given a choice of a similar program at another school, Bennett said.

One parent asked what would happen if a student started a program and found he was not doing well. Bennett said changes could be made because the system was flexible.

"The whole system is built and designed to fit individuals," he said.

The Milwaukee Journal by JOURNAL CO., *Reproduced with permission of* JOURNAL CO., *in the format Republish in a book via Copyright Clearance Center.*

TV6
August 12, 9176

Guest Editorial

This week TV6 aired a series of guest editorials drawing attention to the Milwaukee school plan for this September. We are grateful to TV6, and to all local media, for their efforts to inform our citizens about the many unique educational opportunities which will be available in Milwaukee's schools this September.

Our plans to meet the order of the court are unique because they offer citizens voluntary choices rather than mandatory quotas as is the case in many other cities. Participants in our September plan can select in advance the educational programs they desire for their children.

On Sunday evening at 10:30, I will be reporting to the community how we stand at the mid-point of our recruiting efforts for September. All Milwaukee television stations will carry the Sunday program. At that time, we will know what still has to be done before school starts on September 7.

With the cooperation of the total community, I am confident that by September we will successfully complete the first phase of our three-year plan to improve racial balance in our schools. I firmly believe that by working together we will have school spirit and community pride.

Delivered by Dr. Lee McMurrin, Superintendent of Milwaukee Public Schools

WTMJ Television WTMJ Radio WKTI-FM
August 30, 1976

Comment

Broadcast by Ed Hinshaw

School Superintendent McMurrin says we need to learn to celebrate. And so we do. The Milwaukee schools have voluntarily reached the court mandated goal for the first year of desegregation. More than a third of the city's schools will be racially balanced this fall. And that's worth celebrating.

But, there are two years to go to meet the court order and a week to go to reach the goals set for specialty schools in the city.

So, let's celebrate, but let's also redouble our efforts to make voluntarism work. Look at the specialty schools; learn about the programs. Remember that the second and third years of desegregation are coming. Let's commit ourselves to celebrating success in years two and three by volunteering now.

(Courtesy of WTMJ)

Milwaukee Sentinel
August 5, 1976

Pact OK'd To Transport City Pupils

The County Transit Board Wednesday approved an agreement with the Milwaukee School Board to transport about 4,000 junior and senior high school pupils who voluntarily transfer to other city schools as part of desegregation planning.

The agreement will require that the County Transit System use virtually all of its spare buses, meaning new routes or extension of existing ones will be difficult, a transit system official said.

The agreement, worked out in meetings between county and school officials, covers only pupils in the Milwaukee Public Schools. It is the result of Federal Judge John W. Reynolds' integration order.

The bus service is to begin Sept. 7.

Besides regularly scheduled bus service to move the pupils, the county will set up special "express" runs before and after classes.

The special runs will mean, however, that the County Transit System will have to put virtually all of its spare buses, about 20, into service, said Galen C. Larson, assistant operations manager of the system.

As a result, the transit system will be "hard pressed" to extend existing routes or start new ones, Larson said.

The School Board, under the agreement, will issue special free photo identification passes to the eligible pupils. The passes will be good on the express as well as regular county buses Monday through Friday from 6 a.m. to 6:30 p.m.

The School Board will pay the county $2.50 for each pass for each of the weeks for which the pass is issued.

The agreement requires the County Transit System only to provide "sufficient bus service" to accommodate the pupils involved. The county has the option of providing special runs if there is sufficient ridership.

Larson said the county would start the special runs in September and would continue them unless they do not attract a sufficient number of pupils.

The buses on the special runs will make regular stops on the bus routes in the originating school district, such as the North Division High School district, Larson said.

But once the bus gets outside the originating district, it will travel nonstop along present routes to a regular stop near the so-called host school, such as Bay View High School, officials explained. Special buses will not stop directly at schools.

The agreement also authorizes county bus drivers to take away the special passes from pupils "who appear to be improperly using such passes or who are engaged in such serious breaches of discipline as to jeopardize the safety of others."

To allow the School Board sufficient time to prepare the special photo passes, the county system will provide interim passes at no expense to be used by the eligible pupils from Sept. 7 through 17.

The Milwaukee Sentinel by JOURNAL CO., *Reproduced with permission of* JOURNAL CO., *in the format Republish in a book via Copyright Clearance Center.*

Milwaukee Journal
August 31, 1976

Desegregation Plan Working

Despite all the qualifications about how it was achieved and the good reason for uncertainty about the future, the Milwaukee Public Schools' compliance with its first year desegregation order through largely voluntary transfer of pupils is reason for great cheer. Hard work by educators, committed parents and many others throughout the community must be credited for this achievement.

Had the court order to desegregate one-third of the city's schools this fall not been met through voluntary transfers, then the mandatory assignment of students—busing and all—would have been required. White parents who were reluctant to volunteer their children for this first phase of desegregation owe thanks for their immunity from mandatory transfer to the hundreds of black parents who volunteered their children for transfer away from their neighborhood schools. Nearly all of the shifting of students to meet this year's court order was accomplished by black volunteers.

What happens next year remains uncertain. Peaceful integration and success in implementing the educational reforms that have been started this year could reassure more white parents that voluntary transfer next year is in their children's best interest. For, as School Supt. McMurrin points out, "If we cannot do it voluntarily with educational incentives, we are still going to have to racially balance the schools."

The Milwaukee Journal by JOURNAL CO., Reproduced with permission of JOURNAL CO., in the format Republish in a book via Copyright Clearance Center.

Milwaukee Journal
May 3, 1976

School Board Fumbling Chance

The school desegregation ruling issued last January by Federal Judge Reynolds gave Milwaukee, and particularly the School Board, a remarkable opportunity to devise its own plan to comply with the Constitution. Not many communities under order to desegregate have had such wide leeway to make their own plans. It now appears, however, that the board may forfeit the chance.

One of the key findings of the court was that Milwaukee's open enrollment policy—which lets a student go to any school in the city if it is not overcrowded—had contributed to segregation of schools. It is logical, and probably necessary legally, that this open enrollment policy be abandoned. School Supt. McMurrin recommended that transfers be permitted only if they increased racial integration.

School Board committees have now rejected that, over the advice not only of McMurrin but also of the board's own attorney. Some other key aspects of McMurrin's proposal for compliance with the court also were rejected. This is more than just an indication that the board wants to defy Reynolds; it also runs contrary to the board's own Statement on Education and Human Rights, which pledges to consider all decisions in light of the statement's asserted goal of working toward a more integrated society.

One board member supporting the move to water down McMurrin's plan ironically argued that moving too fast might lead the community to riot. If there is anything to be learned from the way things were mishandled in such places as Boston, however, it is that the greater chance for orderly desegregation occurs when a community devises its own plan, instead of having one imposed by the court.

There has been serious question whether McMurrin's largely voluntary plan could produce enough desegregation to bring Milwaukee into compliance with the Constitution. A watered down version of McMurrin's ideas almost certainly would not. But if that is what the board offers, then the board will be virtually inviting the court to devise and impose a desegregation plan of its own.

It is high time the School Board takes its desegregation opportunity seriously. In fact, it could be the board's last chance to do so.

The Milwaukee Journal by JOURNAL CO., Reproduced with permission of JOURNAL CO., in the format Republish in a book via Copyright Clearance Center.

Milwaukee Journal
April 28, 1976

McMurrin-Board Rift Evident

By David I. Bednarek
of the Journal Staff

A growing split between the Milwaukee School Board and Supt. Lee R. McMurrin over school desegregation plans for September was evident Wednesday.

Board committees, scheduled to act on portions of the plan Monday and Tuesday nights, postponed all action until the weekend after they have received McMurrin's answers on some of their concerns.

Some board members objected Tuesday night to McMurrin's proposal to change the open enrollment policy, saying his proposal was too inflexible.

McMurrin said the changes were needed because the present policy allowed too much racial segregation as integration and was a violation of the Federal Court order banning all forms of discrimination.

North Dispute

Earlier, board members had objected to McMurrin's proposal to close the old North Division High School, a move McMurrin says is necessary if the new school is to open as a racially integrated school in 1978.

Board members also have criticized McMurrin's proposals to bus more black students than whites and McMurrin's selection of career training programs for certain schools.

Board critics went beyond the substance of the plans Tuesday night and criticized the tactics of the administration.

Leon Todd said he would like to discuss some of the information and policy questions being passed between school administrators and John A. Gronouski, the special master appointed by the court to oversee desegregation planning here.

Reports Sought

Lorraine Radtke said she wanted reports of meetings between David Bennett, McMurrin's assistant superintendent who is in charge of desegregation planning, and John Gilligan, Gronouski's assistant.

She said the two were meeting almost daily and the public was getting suspicious of what they were doing.

"This does not say we don't trust anyone," she said. "It does say we want to know what in the hell is going on."

McMurrin, defending his open administration, said the meetings were not secret meetings, but staff meetings, and were not usually recorded in minutes. He agreed, though, to give board members reports on all future meetings between Bennett and Gilligan.

Board to Act

The board is scheduled to act on McMurrin's plan at its meeting next Tuesday, although changes may be made until May 21, the day Gronouski is scheduled to report, on the September plans to Federal Judge John W. Reynolds.

The changes in the open enrollment policy McMurrin wants would prevent black students from transferring to schools that are more than 40% black and would prevent white students from transferring to schools that are more than 60% white.

At present a student may transfer to any school in the city where there is room.

Margaret Dinges said the 40-60 plan is too inflexible. She suggested looking at the possibility of setting the limits at 20-80 for the first year.

The Milwaukee Journal by JOURNAL CO., *Reproduced with permission of* JOURNAL CO.,
in the format Republish in a book via Copyright Clearance Center.

Milwaukee Sentinel
April 28, 1976

Governor Signs Integration Bill

By Neil H. Shively
Sentinel Madison Bureau

Madison, Wis. – A voluntary school integration measure expected to have its greatest impact in the Milwaukee area was signed into law Tuesday by Gov. Lucey.

The bill, AB 1040, appropriates about $5 millions to provide financial incentives designed to encourage participation in the plan.

It was a compromise plan developed by Rep. Dennis Conta (D-Milwaukee), Rep. Rod Johnson (R-Fox Point) and Sen. F. James Sensenbrenner (R-Shorewood).

Lucey used his item veto powers in three places in signing the bill, known in its original form as the Conta Plan.

He struck from it a provision intended to exclude the costs of special transfer programs from the state imposed school cost controls.

Lucey said appeal procedures are available to exceed the cost control and would aid in identifying program costs.

A second veto deleted a section to exclude tuition payments received under the plan from operational receipts for computing general school aid.

Otherwise, Lucey said, the state would pay general aid on those receipts.

The third veto struck a provision basing aid to the transferring district "throughout the period of transfer." Lucey said the language would be administratively unfeasible.

Besides the chief sponsors of the legislation, Milwaukee School Supt. Lee McMurrin and Milwaukee officials were present for the ceremony.

Lucey noted that Milwaukee area officials have already taken steps toward creating planning councils to develop cooperative local transfer programs.

The legislation, he said, permits Wisconsin to exercise "great leadership" in dealing with a problem that has caused trouble in other parts of the country – namely forced busing dictated by Federal Court ordered school integration.

"Through this nationally significant legislation, state government can be – and I hope will be – a supportive partner in what must be primarily a local effort," Lucey said.

State aid will be provided, he said, for the full cost incurred by districts in transporting and providing programs for the students.

Lucey pointed to the voluntary nature of the program, which permits transfers only with the consent of the districts, the students and their parents.

Besides the Milwaukee area, the measure has possible implications in the Ashland, Beloit, Crandon, Kenosha, Racine, Superior and Waukesha areas.

Sensenbrenner said after the signing ceremony that he disliked the item veto that struck the exemption from cost controls which limit school budget increases to 9.5%.

He said he hoped the Legislature would override the veto when it meets here in June in a veto session.

The Milwaukee Sentinel by JOURNAL CO., *Reproduced with permission of* JOURNAL CO., *in the format Republish in a book via Copyright Clearance Center.*

Milwaukee Journal
July 7, 1976

Reynolds OKs Plan for School Integration

Federal Judge John W. Reynolds ordered the Milwaukee School Board Wednesday to carry out the desegregation plan it had previously approved for September.

Reynolds told the attorney for the School Board to draw up the plan and submit it to the other parties in the case within a day or two. They would then have an opportunity to respond to the order and negotiate changes if necessary.

Reynolds also lifted the injunction on construction and remodeling of four schools, 21st Street, Burger, Riverside and Rufus King. He indicated he might lift the injunction on construction of the new Vincent High School on the Northwest Side as soon as the school's impact on integration was determined.

Before Reynolds' order, an attorney for the plaintiffs, Irvin Charne, told Reynolds that the plan had been unanimously approved by attorneys for both sodes. Reynolds responded:

"It makes it a little difficult for the court to disapprove it then, doesn't it?"

The School Board's plan calls for desegregating 66 of the city's 158 schools by September through the creation of several magnet schools designed to attract students voluntarily from throughout the city.

The plan also provides for involuntary transferring students if not enough volunteer. Each of the 68 schools would be between 25% and 45% black, within 10 percentage points of the systemwide black percentage of 35%.

Reynolds ordered last month that one-third of the schools be desegregated by September, one-third in 1977 and one-third in 1978.

He said some questions raised Wednesday with changing the racial quotas and adding more magnet schools in 1977 would be decided later. Reynolds ordered the teachers' union to negotiate with the board on its objections to the administration's plans for in-service training.

Lloyd Barbee, another attorney for the plaintiffs, said during his presentation Wednesday that it was absolutely essential that the staffs and teachers be desegregated with the students this fall.

He said he agreed with the attorney for the School Board, Laurence C. Hammond Jr., who said the school administration should have the authority to assign teachers to the magnet schools to make sure that the staffs are racially integrated.

Hammond said the School Board needed the authority because some teachers with seniority might choose to teach in a particular alternative school just because it was close to home.

The Milwaukee Teachers Education Association, the teachers' union, had suggested a staff integration plan based on voluntary transfers and desegregation through resignations and promotions.

Reynolds indicated that he would order the School Board to spend about $3.5 million that it carried over from its 1975 budget to pay for the desegregation.

The city attorney has said that the School Board cannot use that money until 1977 because state law prohibits such an expenditure.

Reynolds said he felt that the Boston desegregation case indicated that the surplus could be spent. Hammond agreed: "I'm certain the court has the authority."

Reynolds also asked Barbee what he

thought about the School Board's request for more flexibility in the 25% to 45% black ratio Reynolds ordered for all the schools. School officials said the standard would be difficult to meet as elementary school enrollment in the city approaches or passes a 50% minority enrollment.

Barbee said the ratio ordered should be retained until school officials knew exactly what the racial makeup would be.

The present school desegregation plan was approved by the School Board last week after months of disagreement over how to desegregate the schools. The plan was later endorsed by the attorneys for both sides in the suit as well as the city's two congressmen, Henry S. Reuss and Clement J. Zablocki.

The Milwaukee Journal by JOURNAL CO., Reproduced with permission of JOURNAL CO., in the format Republish in a book via Copyright Clearance Center.

www.ingramcontent.com/pod-product-compliance
Lightning Source LLC
Chambersburg PA
CBHW071928290426
44110CB00013B/1522